Cover picture by GregDiesel Photography
Currituck, North Carolina

Contents

Chapter 1	January	pg 1
Chapter 2	February	pg 13
Chapter 3	March	pg 23
Chapter 4	April	pg 33
Chapter 5	May	pg 43
Chapter 6	June	pg 53
Chapter 7	July	pg 63
Chapter 8	August	pg 77
Chapter 9	September	pg 87
Chapter 10	October	pg 97
Chapter 11	November	pg 107
Chapter 12	December	pg 119

In Closing | | pg 133

Introduction

This began as an avenue of venting of frustration with some issues I had been dealing with over a period of several years. There was ten years in a divorce and custody battle and a year after closure on that I found myself a target in a frivolous business lawsuit; which lasted another three years. I survived and overcame both of those; but, at a serious consequence. I also became involved in the politics of an organization and saw a very negative side of people. At a certain point I found myself with a bit more time on my hands and still had a need to communicate with others. I also felt a passion to help others and give hope to those who were struggling with issues in their lives.

I found if I began my day with positive thoughts and let go of the negative, my days were a lot better. I also began praying a lot more and my faith in God seemed to grow. I began to let God take over the issues that needed more resources than I had to give. I found the issues I let go of, were eventually remedied without my doing anything. It was not easy to let go and leave those issues to someone else; however, the more I tried, the easier it became. I also learned; worrying did nothing to help me with the situations.

I am not a writer. I have always enjoyed writing and reading, just never considered it as a profession. I began writing daily notes or messages on the internet. Almost immediately, I began hearing from those who enjoyed reading something upbeat and uplifting first thing in the morning. I also began hearing from people struggling with issues. Most people just wanted someone to talk with about their issues and encouragement. Some people wanted advice and some really had some serious issues which needed help.

I am not perfect by any stretch of the imagination. I also struggled in my life by persistently, having to do things "my way." My first, memorable and notable, experience of doing things "my way"; rather than God's way, goes back some forty-four years. I did not understand the depth of those few minutes; however, they have stayed with me since the young age of 16. I have never mentioned this particular situation before and will spare you the details. Let me just say; "if you ever feel God is talking to you or is trying to tell you something; pay close attention and do what he is saying or what you feel he is leading you to do." To do otherwise, may be allowing the biggest opportunity of your life to slip by and the consequences may follow you for many years. Doing things "my way" gave me the opportunity to understand the difficulties people would and could experience in their lives. Watching and listening to others was also a good way to learn. Self help, spiritual, and psychology books made up most of my library in my younger days. I am just an average person who has been blessed with a persistence to help as many in the world as I can; whether, I know you or not. There are a great many struggling these days, financially as well as personally. It is not always because of the choices or decisions made of the person doing the struggling.

What I have personally learned, over the years this project has taken; has not been anything earth shattering to me. It has opened my eyes more to the enjoyment of life. I am fine tuning and improving some areas of my life and personality; which, I felt needed some work. I will continue to work on those areas. We are, or should be, in a constant state of change, improvement and advances, in our lives. My faith has grown. My faith in God has grown immensely. Since learning to let go of things more often, I have noticed a certain amount of peace; which, I have not had since I was a child. Life in this present world can be complicated, as well as chaotic at times. People seem to be doing too much at one time and letting the "smelling of the flowers" fall to the side. Family time is hurt, and the bonds of the family unit are getting thinner and thinner.

I hope you enjoy the messages here and are able to appreciate the dry sense of humor from time to time. I hope this helps you find some more peace in your life, enjoyment in your life and the ability to forgive those who need to be forgiven. I also hope and pray this may touch the hearts of some who are sitting on the fence; in regards, to God. For those who do not believe and this changes your life, I would love to hear back from you. Trust me, you were created for a reason and have a special purpose in this world. I hope you may find that purpose after reading this book.

Thank you and may God bless you and your family!

Dave Craft

GOOD MORNING!

January 1:
GOOD MORNING! Happy New Year's Day to everyone! Here's hoping and a prayer everyone made it safely home last night. Even with all the blessings of the past year; there are a lot of heartaches and hardships for many. Some families lost loved ones, some had financial difficulties and some are, or had, medical issues. Do not feel like you are alone in your suffering. Many suffer everyday. Just like losing a loved one, you never get over some pain. You just learn to deal with it better. This is what we need to do in life. Do what you can to move your life forward everyday. This year will have ups and downs. It is how you deal with the downs that will dictate how you feel this year. Get rid of the negative in your life and fill the void with positive. Talk to God about your children, your life and the direction he wants you to go. Do not wait until it is too late. We really need to come together as a country. We will not be able to do that unless we come together spiritually also. Help those you can this year. Speak to those you pass. It is only by the grace of God you have the mental and physical abilities you do. That can all change in a blink of an eye. Do not be so foolish as to think you are perfect or invincible. There will come a time when you call on God. You should get on his better side now. I pray this is a great and prosperous year for you. May your health be good and your heart be filled with the joy it was meant to have! Go ahead and get this year started and make this year count! Go get it! It is your first gift of the new year!

January 2:
GOOD MORNING! Go ahead and get this year started! Have a little prayer before moving to far into the day. Recognize the important things and the things that are the most valuable. Those are the things which cannot be bought. Do not believe everything you hear. Seek wisdom for your decisions. May this be a blessed day for you and your loved ones. May this year bring you prosperity, good health and patience to deal with the issues that may arise. Enjoy this day and all it has to offer! Go ahead and get the party started! This party is for you!

January 3:
GOOD MORNING! Congratulations! You have been given a new 1 day! This special gift is a chance to make this a special day for yourself, your loved ones and anyone else you may wish to touch! You are an equal when we come into this world. You will not be

remembered for the material things you leave. Your reputation, character and acts are how people will remember you. Be humble, be kind, be patient and be generous in dealing with others. You have the power to leave a great memory today. Do not allow this opportunity to pass. Do something special for just one person today! Make only good things happen today! Say a prayer and get the day started!

January 4:
GOOD MORNING! Want to wish you a great day today and remind you to think before speaking; especially, when you have felt offended by someone's comment or actions. It is usually better to walk away when angered, rather than saying something you will regret. Once those words come out, they cannot be put back! It is always better to speak with another in a calm tone! Best wishes and prayers for a great year! Please be kind to others and help others when you can! Enjoy this day! Now, go ahead and get the party started!

January 5:
GOOD MORNING! People have a tendency of believing you are the same as the people you associate with. If they lie, chances are good you may also be known as someone who cannot be trusted. If your friends think they are better than everyone else you may also have the same reputation. Choose your friends and your associates carefully. They may effect more than you think! Hope this a good day for you! Praying it is a safe day and you are able to return to all your family members today! Enjoy this day, it is a gift! Go ahead and get the party started!

January 6:
GOOD MORNING! It's a new day! Congratulations! This is a gift! It is your choice what you make of it and what kind of a day it will be! You can wallow in unhappiness and despair or put the negative aside and move forward in your life with your future! Do not let the past hold you back. It is up to you. Life is short! Live it to it's fullest! Help others when you can. Speak to those you pass and respect others. You are needed and you are loved! Make this day count like no other! Go ahead and get this party started! It's yours!

January 7:

GOOD MORNING! Today is a great day to deal with any issues you may have. The anticipation of dealing with a situation or an issue, is, in many cases, worse than dealing with the issue. Sometimes you might need to seek out guidance or wisdom to help you with more delicate situations. Be selective about where you get your wisdom and guidance from. Seek out someone who is older, wiser and may have experienced your situation already. There is no one older, wiser or more experienced than God. Deal with the issue, do not let it get worse than it is! Make the best of this day! It is a gift! Make the best of every minute! Go ahead and get the party started! Enjoy the day!

January 8:

GOOD MORNING! Congratulations on this great gift of a new day! Make this a great day for yourself. Let go of any hard feelings you may be harboring towards others. Spend your time on positive thoughts, plans and goals. Move on! May this be a blessed day for you and your loved ones. May your travels be safe and your health good. Make the best of every minute. You just do not know when your last minute may arrive. Enjoy your day! Let your loved ones know you love them! It is your day! Treat it like the gift it is! Go get it!

January 9:

GOOD MORNING! Congratulations on your newest day! Today may bring some bad news, some negative issues or some disappointments. There may even be some people who intentional want to hurt you. Under a false pretext of feeling better about themselves. Sometimes people will go out of their way to demean others. Unfortunately, in reality there is not much you can do with people like this except ignore them and move on. Reality does not have a delete button. You have to learn to deal with these people to a certain extent. Understand that people who hurt others are generally troubled people, in some way. You are not here to hurt others. You are here to help others. Unfortunately that act is not as common as it has been in the past. Spend your time with positive people doing positive things! Life is short. Be happy in it! Make every minute count in this day! Let those you care about know you care! Enjoy the day and go get it! It is a gift!

January 10:

GOOD MORNING! Welcome to the first day of the rest of your life! Today is the day you can accept the path you are on or change the direction of your life! The change does not have to be big; however, just a change in your schedule or a slight change in the start to your day is all that is needed to get the ball rolling. Start the day with a walk or music rather than the news. Change your breakfast. Call or leave a note for someone special in your life before you leave home. Take a walk for lunch or treat yourself to a special lunch today. At the end of the day, do something different from the regular routine. Have some ice cream or take the kids out for a treat. Find a nice park to sit at for a while. Enjoy the outdoors or stop by your favorite store. Change your routine and do something YOU want to do and enjoy doing! It will feel great! May this be a special day in your life and may something very special and unexpected come your way! Go ahead and get your day started! It is moving on and people need you and love you! Go for it!

January 11:

GOOD MORNING! Here's hoping today you will thank God for your day before the day gets too far along! If you have shot an arrow from a bow; you know that arrow is coming down. You may not know where or when it is coming; however, you know it is coming down. You can aim and calculate to the best of your ability, but that arrow is not always going to end up in the bull's eye. That is kind of how life can be. No matter how hard you plan or calculate; things just do not always end up where they were planned. You can never plan for all the contingencies in life. There are many factors, usually, with every decision you make. When an arrow misses a target the shooter spends some time looking for the arrow. Life is the same way. When things do not go as planned, time is spent trying to understand why something happened or trying to get things to go in another direction. Just like the shooter does not give up, you just have to continue moving forward with your goals and making another plan for that next day, week, month or even years. You just never give up! Change your plans, change your direction, change your friends or change your schedule if that helps. Just keep moving forward and keep your eye on the target or goals. If we always received everything we wanted, when we wanted, life would be too easy and we would not learn to appreciate things. Maybe today is the day you will hit the target! Whatever this day brings to your door, just smile, thank God for the lesson and move on! Go ahead and this day started! It is a gift and it is yours! Enjoy it and make the best of every minute! Get the party started!

January 12:
GOOD MORNING! Just want to tell you how glad it is to see you here today! Just knowing you are here makes me feel better. I just want to say, "I hope today is a great day for you and your loved ones." I hope you are blessed beyond any expectations. You just never know what or who may cross your path in life. There will be some negative and there will be some positive. Pray you have the wisdom to recognize the positive and the ability to turn you back on the negative. May you be blessed and may your heart be filled with the joy it was meant to have! Share your happiness with others and help others whenever you can! This life is short and do not be confused by temporary happiness and the happiness which will last a lifetime! Go ahead and get the party started! Go get it!

January 13:
GOOD MORNING! Today is a gift you have been given. You have been given this gift because your job, or reason for being here has not been completed. One day your purpose here will be completed and you will leave the world. You may not even know when you time comes. Your life in this world may just come to an end. This is why it is always good to let those you care about, know you love them. Tomorrow you may not have that opportunity. May you be blessed with good health, wisdom and a happy heart. Enjoy the day, it is a gift. Help others when you can! Go ahead and get the party started! Know you are loved just the way you are!

January 14:
GOOD MORNING! May this be a great day for you! May you be safe and may your health be good. If you were to leave this world today, how would you be remembered? What would your accomplishments be? Do not let your life be a waste. Help others. Make a difference in someone's life. Enjoy this day. Appreciate the gift God has given you! May God smile on you and bless you and your loved ones

January 15:
GOOD MORNING! So glad to see you today! There are so many
people dealing with stress these days. No matter how hard you try,
there are, probably, going to be days when the stress is greater
than other days. Those are the days when you just have to breathe
deeply and have a little prayer before you leave home. On the days
when unexpected issues arise; you just have think carefully and
slowly before responding. Once you lose your composure and let
hateful words or thoughts fly from your mouth; you may find others do not forget those words or thoughts. May this day bring
something unexpected and special to you! May you and your loved
ones be blessed with good health and wisdom all of your lives.
Help others whenever you can. Speak to those you pass! Go ahead
and get this party started! Go has given you a gift. Make the best
use of every minute!

January 16:
GOOD MORNING! What a great day to be alive! Everyday is a
great day to be alive. Some days are just better than others. Situations that cross our paths are no worse or better than we make
them. It is not the act which effects our emotions. It is the way we
deal with our own emotions which makes situations really good,
really bad or neutral. Everyone will experience embarrassing moments, situations which will hurt or anger in their lifetime. Your
response may be remembered long after the situation has passed.
Choose your words carefully and slowly. Never respond in anger.
Walking away is usually better than an angry response. Speak
kindly to everyone. Even those who have tried to hurt you. Positive
consequences follow positive behavior. This day is a gift for you.
Make the most of every minute of this day. Spend it with positive
thoughts and actions. You will be a lot happier at the end of the
day! Get the day started!

January 17:
GOOD MORNING! Hoping you were able to jump out of the bed
this morning! (if not jump, a little roll will work) Also hope you are
looking forward to this day and are looking forward to leading
your day; rather than following in it. Do not wait for others, or
something to happen to get the day started. Get it moving along.
Leave a mark in the world. Treat others well and be kind to people
you meet. You never know who you may be talking too. There is no
glamour or reward in being vindictive, deceptive, or hateful to-

wards others. This goes for business or personal life. Make your own decisions and stand by what you believe. Make this a great day for yourself and your loved ones! Help those you can. Appreciate what you have been given and thank God for this day! It's your party, go ahead and get it started!

January 18:
GOOD MORNING! Let's get this day started! There are people to see, jobs to do, places to be and people to help! Make this a great day for yourself and others around you. Look at how to get the job done. Forget about any hurdles and just move forward. Think of what you can do without any negative thoughts in your mind. Fill your heart with positive and you'll feel better. Fill your mind with positive and you'll do more. Thank God for what you have been given. This is your day and it is up to you how it turns out! Let's get this party started!

January 19:
GOOD MORNING! Occasionally, you are given an opportunity to help someone. The value of the help you give will vary from person to person. Some people may look at the help, as a little. There are others who may consider just a few words the help of a true friend and a life saver. Never pass up the opportunity to help someone. You just never know what that help may mean to that person and how much it may help them.. Then again, occasionally, you may actually see the benefit of your help. Either way, you have done a good thing to benefit someone else. May you and your family be blessed. May today bring something else positive in your life. Never run from a challenge and get your day started. It is your gift!

January 20:
GOOD MORNING! Welcome to the newest day God has given you! Today, you may be given some news you did not want to hear. It may be hurtful. It may be completely unexpected. It may be devastating. It may feel as your world has ended. Most situations are not as bad as they initially seem. Do not let first impressions rule your day. Look hard and you will find the positive. For every negative action there is a positive reaction. May this be the best day of your life. May you touch another's life today and may you be able to help someone. Speak to those you pass and listen to those who may need to express themselves. Your attention may just change

the entire life of someone else. Go ahead and get your party started. The day is moving on and you need to move with it!

January 21:
GOOD MORNING! What a great day to be alive! Your day can be better starting with a little prayer and thanking God for what you have and who you are. A person does not have to look far to see others who are not as fortunate as those around them. Sometimes, when times get tough, it's harder to think about what you have to be grateful for. Everyone has something to be thankful for. It may not always be something tangible. Keep in mind, the most valuable things are things which you cannot put a value on. May this be the greatest day of your life. May something truly special and unexpected come your way! Go ahead and get your party started!

January 22:
GOOD MORNING! Congratulations on your new day! May this be the best day of your life! May something special and unexpected come you way. May you and your loved ones be blessed with good health, wisdom for your decisions, a happy heart and guidance, for direction in your life. Speak only kind words to those you pass and those you speak of. You are special and need to be yourself. Do not waste your time being someone you are not. God made you the way you are. You can improve your attitude; without changing the person. Enjoy this day and all it offers. Go ahead and get your party started!

January 23:
GOOD MORNING! Welcome to your new day! Let today be the day you leave the negative from the past, in the past. Approach today and the challenges it my bring, with an open mind and a positive attitude. If a person could release all the negative they may be carrying around; their accomplishments could be unlimited. Let this be the day your attitude is taken over by all positive thoughts. Look forward to your future with a open mind and a good heart. Extend your hand to those who may not be as fortunate as you. Help those you can. Thank God for who you are and what you have. Be blessed with good health, wisdom and a happy and content heart. This is going to to be a great day, no matter what is thrown your way! Go ahead and get party started! Don't look back!

January. 24:
GOOD MORNING! Make today a great day for yourself and those around you. Take the time to talk to others. Let them know you care. You never know who you will meet. This is a small world. We are here to help each other in this world. Helping others will give you a feeling of true happiness. It can as simple as making a phone call or visiting someone. Sometimes, the best feeling comes from doing something for someone; while, no one knows what you did. Enjoy this day. It is a gift. Thank God for what you have been given. Enjoy this day and make the best of every minute. Go ahead and get your party started!

January 25:
GOOD MORNING! Congratulations on the newest day of your life. Make it a special day for yourself by making it special for others. If you are traveling, take extra time this time of the year. It does not pay to get into a hurry. If it is cold in your area, you may want to be sure you have a blanket and coat in your car, along with a working flashlight. You just never know what the next minute may bring to you, in your life. Enjoy this day as it was meant to be enjoyed. Count your blessings. No matter what the situation in your life is; there is someone out there who would rather be in your shoes than their own. Never go to bed or leave the house angry. May you and your loved ones be blessed! Go ahead and get the party started! It's God gift to you today!

January 26:
GOOD MORNING! It's a new day. How will you be remembered when you pass from this world? Are the memories you leave, going to be good or not so good? Will people remember you as a person who helped others or someone who just did for themselves? We are here to be happy and we are here to help others. You do not have to wait for someone to ask for help. If you see a need, take care of it. Sooner or later, everyone needs help. Many are still close to losing their homes. Jobs are getting harder to find and do not pay as much as they use to. Others need you! May this be a great day for you and your loved ones! Forget the negative and move in a positive direction. God loves you and it would be good to speak to him on occasion. Make this day count! Enjoy ever minute!

January 27:

GOOD MORNING! Today is a good day to be alive! We only have one shot at doing the best we can in this life. Many mistakes are made. Many good decisions are also made. Learn from the mistakes and be humbly grateful for good decisions. There will be set backs. There will also be unexpected surprises. Accept both as lessons in this life. We are here to be happy in this life and at peace with ourselves. You deserve to be happy. It is up to you to have it. Make this a great day for yourself and those around you. May this be the greatest day of your life! Go ahead and get the party started!

January 28:

GOOD MORNING! It is a new day for you! Since it is a new day, it is a good day. Keep you eyes forward and your attitude positive. Turn your back on the negative and those who criticize you. Give everything you do, your best effort. Make every minute count. Give your hand to those who need a hand. Speak kindly to others. Make this a special day for someone else. Thank God for what you have and who you are. May you be blessed with wisdom and good health! Go get this day. It is God's gift to you!

January 29:

GOOD MORNING! Welcome to the first day of the rest of your life! Never give up on your dreams or your goals. You may not always get what you want, when you want. If you stop trying, your chances of seeing your goals or dreams stop too. May this be a special day for you. May you and your loved ones be blessed with wisdom, guidance, good health and compassion towards others. Make this a special day for someone else. Go ahead and get your party started. This day is your gift. Make every minute count!

January 30:

GOOD MORNING! Here is a new day to celebrate and enjoy! Today is a good day to let go of any anger you may be carrying. It does not matter what the anger generated from or how long you may of had it. It is taking up space and time you can be using for positive things. Have you ever known someone to carry a grudge for years and want only to hurt someone in some way? Think of the wasted time which was spent with those negative feelings. It really is sad when you think about the waste; yet, there are people who will wait years, just to say, "I got even." Actually, they will never get even. They had to keep these negative thoughts in the recesses of their mind for much longer than just the few minutes they feel, "I got even." Take a few minutes and talk with God today. He knows you and can give you a peace you may have never known. Use your time wisely and with positive purpose. Make every minute count. Enjoy this day. It is a gift. Let your loved ones know you care. Go ahead and get your party started!

January 31:
GOOD MORNING! Congratulations on your new gift; which is, today. Everyone has a different purpose in this world. There is something God has planned for each person. It may be to help many people. It may be to help one person in their life. Some people will accomplish their goal or purpose early on in life. Some may not complete their purpose for many years of life. The purpose could be as significant as saving another's life or as small as just a phrase you speak which effects someone else's life. Many will know what their purpose was. Many may not ever know what they have done or who they effected. This makes treating others well; so much more important. Speak to everyone you pass. It does not matter what they are wearing or what they look like. At the moment in life when your path crosses another's, you just may be the most important person in their life. Let that moment and memory be a good one. Speak kindly to them and ask how they are. Enjoy this day and touch another's life, in a positive way, today. This day is a gift from God. Treat is as the blessing it is. Go ahead and get your party started!

February 1:
GOOD MORNING! Here's hoping this day is a great success. May you have peace and may something truly special and unexpected come your way. Let those you love, know you care. Speak kindly to everyone. Be slow to anger. Do not let pride be a part of your decisions. Make this a great day for yourself and your loved ones. It is a gift; treat it as the best gift you have ever been given. Enjoy your day and get your party started!

February 2:
GOOD MORNING! So glad to see you today. Today is a great day to put the loved ones first and let them know you care. Call, visit or spend time with those who are most important to you. In the end the loved ones will be the most important parts of your life. They deserve to know how important they are. Enjoy this day and let God know you appreciate your loved ones, as well as this day. Go ahead and get the party started. It is your day!

February 3:
GOOD MORNING! Everyone is born a little different. That little difference gives everyone that special characteristic about themselves. It may be something about your character. It may be an ability to listen to others. It may be a business sense. It may be the ability to work with others. It may be an ability to organize. No matter what that characteristic is; it gives a special ability to help others. Everyone has it. It is up to the individual whether to use it for the purpose it was given, or not. May this be a blessed day for you and your loved ones. Enjoy this day. It is truly a gift from God. Make the best of every minute.

February 4:
GOOD MORNING! Today is a good day to appreciate and thank God for the abilities, physical and mental, you have. You could very easily be one of those who suffer from mental illness, substance abuse, paranoia, or maybe stress from what you might have seen and experienced in life. Never turn you back on another person. Homeless people are someone's brother, sister, aunt, uncle, father, mother, or even grandparent. They are people. Never think yourself so good as to think you could never be in that position. When you see a need, provide an answer. Count your blessings and thank God for what you have. It could change tomorrow. Make every minute of your day count!

February 5:

GOOD MORNING! Make all the minutes of this day count for something positive. Speak kindly to others. Let others know you care about them. Be respectful of yourself and others. Respect has to be earned; it is not a given. Enjoy your day and don't forget a little prayer. Go get it. It's yours!

February 6:

GOOD MORNING! Welcome to your new day! Today is a good time to remember what and/or who is important to you. Many seem to be confused about whether it is the material things; or is the elderly family member or the family member who may not be doing so well because of one reason or another. It is ironic how hard people will work at saving or collecting money or material things. Some will do anything; including hurting others for money or maybe prestige. If they worked as hard, at helping their family members or neighbors overcome hardships they may be facing, the world would be a much greater place. No one is taking their property or material things with them when they pass from this world. Many will see their other family members in the next world. Maybe it is time to really consider what or who is important. Make this a special day for someone. Give and it will come back to you. Pray for others as well as yourself. Be patient with others and let them know you care. May you and your family be blessed today with good health, patience, guidance and wisdom. Enjoy this day and all it brings!

February 7:

GOOD MORNING! Make this a great day for yourself. Turn off the negative. Ignore those who would bring you down emotionally and spiritually. Focus on progress, your goals and the end of your task. Do not allow others to distract you. Do not deviate from your path. Without action, nothing is going to happen. May this be a blessed day for you and your loved ones. May something special come your way today. Pray and pray with your loved ones. This is your day. Go get it and make every minute count!

February 8:

GOOD MORNING! Welcome to your new day. Glad to see you are here. Starting your day with a little prayer and faith can do wonders for removing the stress you may be facing. Leave yesterday in the past and look forward. Do something a little different today. Take a walk, by yourself or with a loved one. Take the time to smell the flowers, hear the rain, feel the wind or just smell the air. Appreciate what you have and what is around you. Go ahead and enjoy your day. It is a gift of God and made special for you. Make the best of every minute. Go ahead and get your party started!

February 9:
GOOD MORNING! Know you are special just the way you are. Be the person God made you to be. Do not try to be someone you are not. Do not try to be a different person for someone else. Be yourself. You are important the way you are. Make the most of every minute of this day. Be kind to others. Speak kindly to those you pass. Help others when you have the opportunity. Let your loved ones know you care.Thank God for who you are and what you have. Go ahead and get your party started! It's your day!

February 10:
GOOD MORNING! You have been given a new day. Today is a great day to let God know you are grateful for what you have been given. Sooner or later, most will turn to God for help with their health or a prayer for someone else. Do not wait until you need him to speak to him. May this be a great day for you and your loved ones. Enjoy this day and leave only good feelings in your path. Know you are loved. May you be blessed.

February 11:
GOOD MORNING! Welcome to the first day of the rest of your life. Start your life off right. Do not just plan things; do things. Make things happen. Do not sit and wait for things to come to you. Set goals and set them high. You can do whatever it is you want to do. Be persistent and keep moving forward. Do not let the hurdles stand in your way. Life is not going to be easy for everyone. Have an appreciation for what you have been given. There are others who would love to have your life. Take the time to meet and learn about others. It may mean everything to one person, on a certain day. Get your new life started. Treat this day as the gift God wanted it to be. Go ahead and get the party started!

February 12:
GOOD MORNING! Today just may be the day you meet someone, you were not expecting, who effects your life. It may be someone

you meet in the line for coffee. It may be someone in a check out line near you. You just never know who is around you. If you do not speak to and meet others you may be missing the best experience of your life. Speak to those you come into contact with. There are some wonderful people out there. You may be missing the best opportunity of your life if you pass up speaking to someone standing next to you. Enjoy this day and make the best of every minute! It is your day! Enjoy it and go get it! It is yours!

February 13:
GOOD MORNING! It's a new day for you to enjoy! It's a great day to be alive. Many people will deal with the passing of a loved one, a family member, a friend or maybe just an acquaintance. Many will be blessed by knowing when a person is going to be leaving this world. They will be able to say goodbye to their loved ones. Many will not be so fortunate. Some will step away from their homes today and never return. Never leave your home angry and never go to bed angry. Do not take a chance on carrying a regretful burden the rest of your life. Life is too short to be angry. Let it go and move on. Make this a happy day for yourself and those around you. May you be blessed. Go ahead and get your party started!

February 14:
GOOD MORNING! It is good to have you here today! Decisions you make will take you in different directions throughout your lives. Many do not have an appreciation of how fragile life is until later in their lives. A privileged few understand how fragile and important life can be. Unfortunately, many have to lose loved ones or suffer from illnesses during their lives to have this appreciation. Please consider how life would be without certain loved ones in your life. Do not wait until others are gone before telling them you care. Appreciate those who appreciate you. Know you are loved and special. Be yourself and help others when you can. May this be the best day of your life. May you be blessed with wisdom and guidance. Go ahead and get this day started. It is your party!

February 15:
GOOD MORNING! It's so good to see you. Today I would just like to ask that you let those you care about, know you care about them. There is no guarantee when you or your loved ones leave home today, you will return.   Today, there are children or adults who will not make it home. The cause will not be anything they

planned on. People may be on their knees today begging to have their family members back or for help. Do not wait until you need God to talk with him. He knows you. He wants to hear from you. Life is already short. Appreciate every minute you have. May you and your loved ones be blessed with good health, guidance, wisdom and good health.

February 16:
GOOD MORNING! It's a great day to be alive. Let go of the anger you may be carrying and enjoy more of your day. Let go of any negative feelings you have towards others and enjoy more of your day. The more positive you have in your life, the happier you will be. The more positive you have in your life the more successful you will be. The more positive you have in your life the more forward you can move. You are here to be happy. It is up to you whether that is the way you will live your life, or not. Have faith in yourself and trust in God for guidance. Make it happen. It is up to you. Go ahead and get your day started!

February 17:
GOOD MORNING! Be yourself today. Do not allow other's attitudes or feelings to hurt you. You are special and you are loved for who you are. Make this a great day for yourself and your loved ones. Today is a good day to let God know you think about him. May you be blessed beyond your expectations and dreams. It is your day. Go get it!

February 18:
GOOD MORNING! It's a new day and it's your day. It's up to you how this day will be. No matter what comes your way your attitude will dictate how good or bad it is. Many have a tendency to overreact to situations. No matter what reaction you have or what the situation is, once it has happened nothing you do is going to reverse it. The only thing left is how you deal with the aftermath. Tomorrow is another day and you may learn a lesson; so repair what you can and move on. Make the best of this day. Everyday is a gift. Give someone a reason to have a positive memory of this day. Doing for others always makes a person feel good. Enjoy this day and go ahead and get your party started!

February 19:
GOOD MORNING! Finally, a new day and a new start to the rest of your life. If things were not quite how you would like, yesterday; leave them in the past, forget them and start new today! The only thing holding you back, is yourself. We are in this world to be productive and happy. It's up to you to have that. Everyone makes mistakes. No one is perfect. Learn from your mistakes and continue to move forward. Never give up. Make this a great day. Surround yourself with positive feelings and thoughts. Thank God for the gift of this new day and make the best of this gift! Go get it. It is only going to be as good as you make it!

February 20:
GOOD MORNING! With so many people occupying positions they are not qualified for, there are a lot more bad decisions being made. People will do about anything to make others look bad, and themselves good. It is a false security to act like this. Do not be taken in by the immature and insecure behavior of people. Be bigger. Think before you allow your emotions to control your reactions. Seek guidance for your decisions. Only a fool thinks they have all the answers. Make the best of every minute and let your loved ones know you care. Enjoy this day. It is a gift from God! Go ahead and get the party started!

February 21:
GOOD MORNING! Isn't it a great day to be alive? Even with the issues people may be having; today is a great day. You have to appreciate all that you have. All the physical and mental capabilities you have is a wonderful place to start. Do not let the immature actions or behavior of others effect you. Time catches up to everyone. There are consequences for our actions; whether positive or negative. Be kind to others, speak to those you pass. Help others whenever you can. You might be amazed at how good helping others will make you feel. Make the best of every minute and enjoy this day. It is a gift from God. Go ahead and get your party started!

February 22:
GOOD MORNING! One of the greatest feelings in this world comes from helping others and seeing the happiness they get from your gift. It does not have to be money or something tangible. It

can be something as simple as a phone call or just a little of your time to listen to someone who has no one else to talk with. So many elderly people live in nursing homes and they just go from day to day without anyone to talk with or anyone to share things with. Some may be mentally disadvantaged. You may have a friend, or a loved one, who is having a hard time right now. Just give others a little of your time. It may be you one day who needs that special friend. May you be blessed with good health, guidance, wisdom and compassion towards others. Help others with the gifts you have been given. Make the best of every minute and help others when you can. It is your day. Make the best of it.

February 23:
GOOD MORNING! It feels so good to be here another day. No matter what situations there may come today, it is a good day to be alive. Spend some time with your loved ones. Set aside some time for something you like to do. Make the best of every minute of this day. Be happy and be grateful for what you have and have been given. May God bless you and your family..Let this be a great day!

February 24:
GOOD MORNING! "Dear Heavenly Father, Thank you for this day you have given us. Thank you for allowing us to live in this Christian nation where we still have the freedoms we do. Thank you for the food we have. Thank you for the shelter we have. Thank you for all you have given us, Lord. Most especially, thank you for the great gift of salvation you have offered and given to us all; through the blood of your son. I pray for those who have not opened their hearts and minds to you Lord. May they hear the words that will lead them to accept you as their savior. May they accept the gift of salvation you have offered before they pass from this world. Father, I ask that you watch over everyone today and take them to their destinations safely and allow them to return home. Lay your healing hands on those who are ill and those who are troubled. Please, bless us all with good health, wisdom, patience, forgiveness, understanding and compassion towards others. Guide us and help us to make the right decisions today. Forgive us for our sins and have mercy on our souls. In Jesus name I pray and ask for these things. Amen."

February 25:

GOOD MORNING! Glad to see you have another day. It's time to shake the negative out of the head. Get that coffee, tea or drink down. Let's get this day rocking and rolling. It is just a great day to be here. Let your loved ones know you care and spend a few minutes with them. Have a little breakfast and maybe you can start that next coffee as you get ready for this day. Make sure your pets are taken care of and it's time to get moving into a new day. Make it count and help others when you can. Let go of the issues from yesterday and know it is a new day. Let those you care about know you love them. Get a little prayer in and let's get the party started! Do not let anyone or anything hold you back. It is up to you. Go for it!

February 26:

GOOD MORNING! Welcome to the first day of the rest of your life. You have a new day!. Open up the curtains, get that coffee, or whatever it is which helps open the little peepers up, and lets get the day moving! You cannot go wrong starting the day with a little prayer, a little time with the loved ones and maybe a little healthy breakfast. Be safe today, be kind to others, help anyone you can and enjoy every minute of this day. Go ahead and get the party started. It is yours!

February 27:

GOOD MORNING! When you think of all those moments from your past that you wish you can change; remember those moments and situations are part of what brought you to where you are now. Live and learn. Enjoy your day and make it special for your loved ones. Make the most of every minute of this day. It is a gift. Go ahead and get your party started.

February 28:

GOOD MORNING! So glad you are here to see another day. During your life you will come across many people. Some of those will be friends and some will want to call themselves friends. Very few will really be true "friends." You will learn as you go which ones are truly worth calling "friends." There will be some disappointments. Do not let those disappointments effect your feelings towards others. Life will be full of ups and downs. You are to be happy in this world. Keep this in mind as you go through the day.

You are loved and you are needed. Go ahead and get the party started. It is a gift!

March 1:

GOOD MORNING! Welcome to your newest day. It is all yours to make as good as you want it. The worse of situations can be much better with the right attitude. Often, the more a person talks, the worse the situation will become. To continually argue with another is pointless and produces a strong possibility of damaged relationships. State your position and let it go. Pick and choose your battles wisely. Let your loved ones know you care and spend time with them. Make the best of everyday. Go ahead and get this party started!

March 2:

GOOD MORNING! It is a great day to be alive. You have been created special in your own way. It is God's gift to you. He has a special plan for everyone, including you. God wants you to be successful and happy in your life. If you feel your life is lacking something or issues are overcoming you; a prayer may just be what you need. You can do that anywhere at anytime. Do not keep putting it off. You will only have so many chances. Enjoy this gift of a day. Make it a special day for yourself and loved ones!

March 3:

GOOD MORNING! May this be a great day for you. Go ahead and get that coffee down and get the day started. Take a little extra time for yourself today and take a walk or just sit outside and see the beautiful land you live in. Share your day and happiness with others. Speak to those you pass and help others when you can. May you and yur loved ones be blessed with good health, wisdom, patience and compassion. Go ahead and get the party started!

March 4:

GOOD MORNING! Let this be a great day for yourself. Be kind to others, Speak kindly to those you pass. Never let an opportunity to meet someone go by. You never know who it may be. When you speak to others, about others, you never know who you may be speaking of either. Be remembered for being kind to others; not forgotten for what you took. Have an excellent day. Share it with others.

March 5:

GOOD MORNING! It is so good to see you are here today. May today be a great day for you and your loved ones. May something special and unexpected come your way today. May you and your loved ones have good health and may you be protected from harm. Just a thought; if there was a disaster in your area, whether natural or man made, does your family have a plan where to go or meet? Do your children know what to do, if something happened to you today? Something to think about and maybe talk about with the children. Fear is the worst of all emotions. Many adults have a hard time with the unknown or fear; for children it can make things so much worse. Having some kind of plan in place may make things a lot easier for them. Have a great day and make every minute of today count. You do have a purpose in being here and you are loved!

March 6:
GOOD MORNING! It is a great day to be you. These days it is not unusual to feel stressed or frustrated. Do not feel like you are the only one with these feelings. People's lives are changing through no fault, or activity, of their own. Most of the issues which people have to face; turn out to be not so big when the emotion is taken out of the picture. Think before you react. Give all your decisions serious consideration before responding. Do not be afraid to seek guidance or help with your decisions. Do not feel just anyone can give good advice. No one knows everything. May this be a great day for you. It is up to you how good you can make it. May your health be good and your heart filled with the joy your were meant to have. Get your day started and do not waste a minute of your time!

March 7:
GOOD MORNING! Today is a great day to consider how you will be remembered when you leave this world. Is your character going to be well thought of? Are you going to leave some positive actions in your wake. Will people remember good things you did or will you be forgotten quickly? Your memory will be your legacy. Leave something good in your past. Help others when you can and be compassionate towards others. Make the best of this day and make this day your best. It is up to you. Go get it and make it count!

March 8:
GOOD MORNING! It's a new day and it is a gift to you. Everyday you have is a gift. Everyday you have is a day you need to appreciate and make it the best you can. You only have one chance at

every day. Tomorrow is not a guarantee. When you leave this world, you will not be taking anything with you. Take care of your loved ones when you are here and help those you can when can. Let those you care about know you care. Make this the best day you can. You are here to be happy, successful and compassionate to others. Thank God for this gift of a new day. You may want to take the time to say, "Thank you." It is a good time to get the party started!

March 9:
GOOD MORNING! May this be a good day for you and your loved ones. May you be blessed with good health, wisdom, patience and compassion towards others. May something unexpected and rewarding come your way. Material things come and go in your life. Material things can be replaced. Your loved ones cannot. Treat them as the gold they are. Enjoy this day and do not look back. It's all yours, just go get it!

March 10:
GOOD MORNING! Welcome to the newest day of your life! Today you have the opportunity to let those you love know you care about them. You also have the opportunity to thank God for what you have been given. Tomorrow you may not have the opportunity for either. In the blink of an eye; lives change, everyday. Live your life to it's fullest. Be kind to others and share whatever you can to help others. Forgive others and do not carry anger with you. Life is too short to spend time on the negative. Go ahead and get your new day started. What you make of it is up to you. Enjoy this day. It is a gift from God!

March 11:
GOOD MORNING! It seems like everyday people are being hit with issues through no fault of their own. It may be financial, health, personal, business, maybe even family. The attitude people have when dealing with these issues can make things a lot worse or not so bad. When things seem to be going bad, think about your reaction before your let something come flying out of your mouth. Once it comes out, you cannot put it back. Be patient with your emotions. Things usually are not as bad as they may feel. Enjoy your day and spend time with your family and loved ones. In the end, they are really what matters. Make the best of this day and enjoy every minute!

March 12:
GOOD MORNING! Today is a new day for you. Everyday you are here is a day less in your future. It is always better to plan ahead and that includes what happens when you pass from this world. People do not like talking about this or facing the reality of it. Many people make arrangements ahead of time to save others from having to do it afterwards. Imagine how much less stress a child might feel if their parents had discussed their loss with them. Those who have pets, should make arrangements for someone to take care of the furry family members. You just never know what may happen during your day. Your life can change in the blink of an eye. Help your loved ones by planning your future as much as possible. One last thought; are you going to be remembered for what you did for others or what you did to others? Enjoy this day as the gift it is! Make the best of every minute and go get it!

March 13:
GOOD MORNING! Today is a wonderful time to be alive. May this be a great day for you and your loved ones. May you be blessed with something unexpected. Be grateful for what you have and what you have been given. It is always good to thank God for who you are and what you have! Appreciate this day day. It is a gift,,May you be blessed with good health and be protection from harm. Get your party started!

March 14:
GOOD MORNING! Welcome to the first day of the rest of your life. It's a new day to enjoy like no other day you ever have. Take the time to enjoy your loved ones and spend time with them if possible. Maybe you can take the time to enjoy the sound of the wind in the trees, the birds, the waves of a pond or lake, or maybe even the sound of a flowing river. Appreciate what is around you and the gift of the senses you have. Let this be the best day of your life!

March 15:
GOOD MORNING! Congratulations, you have been given a new day to enjoy and spread that enjoyment to others. One item every individual is personally responsible for; is the outcome of their own character and integrity. No one can hurt that except the owner. It cannot be taken from you. It pays to be honest and maintain a good character along with integrity. Those are the people who you can trust and want as friends. Do something special for some-

one today. Enjoy this gift of a day! Go ahead and get your party started!

March 16:
GOOD MORNING! May this be a great day for you. May you make a new friend today. A true friend is someone who stands beside you in the tough times as well as the good. Someone who cares what you have to say and how you feel. There are a lot of good people out there. To meet them, you have to talk to them. Get to know others. Many of those good people are really special people. Take the time to know others. Enjoy this day. It is a gift from God. Go get it. It is for you to enjoy...

March 17:
GOOD MORNING: Looks like you will get to join the rest of the world today! Congratulations and welcome to your new day. Everyone is different and everyone has a different opinion. Some of the subjects of these opinions may be very important; some not so much. Different opinions bring disagreements which can turn into arguments. Not all arguments are worth the time and energy spent. Spend your time on positive thoughts and actions. If you feel you must be involved then choose your battles carefully. Be sure there is something positive to come from the disagreement. Enjoy this day. It is a gift.

March 18:
GOOD MORNING! It is a new day for you. Make it a great day. No matter what comes your way, just calmly deal with it and move on. Chances are the issues seem a lot worse than they are. Do not allow your emotions to control your actions. That is a sure way to develop regrets. Learn from those issues. You were given this day as a gift. Enjoy it and get your party started!

March 19:
GOOD MORNING! Welcome to the newest day of your life. At some point in your life the question of "why you are here" should cross your mind. Everyday, is a day less in your life and a day less to accomplish your purpose in this life. Some may be here for many different accomplishments. Some may be here for just one or two great moments. Not everyone will be recognized for what they do or what they accomplish. Everyone has a purpose in this world. May your life be complete and may your purpose be real-

ized. Whatever you do today, do it well. May this also be a great day for you. Make the day count May you feel fulfilled and may you be content. Get your party started. It is a gift!

March 20:
GOOD MORNING! Good to see you today. It may not seem like it; however, today is a special day. First, this day is a gift from God. Next, there are people who depend on your presence in this world. There are also people who love you and need you. Some may need to see you and/or hear your voice on a regular basis. The bottom line is you are important. Remember this as you go through your day. People look to you for comfort, advice, or maybe just attention. Let yourself be available to others who need you. You may need someone one day. May this be a blessed day for you and your loved ones. May you be protected from harm and given wisdom and guidance for your decisions. May your health be good and life, long. Enjoy your day and make the best of every minute. Go ahead and get your party started!

March 21:
GOOD MORNING! Today is a new day for you. Along with being given a new day to spend with your loved ones; this is a day you have to take advantage of the time you have been given. You can make others happy, whether you know them or not. You can give joy to others no matter how they feel, and you can do good for others without being asked. This day and what you accomplish is up to you. Be glad in being here and having what you have. Share your joy with others and do it with a smile. There are others who would give anything to be as well off as you, no matter what you think. May you be blessed today like you have never been before and may you bless others with your happiness and joy. It is your day and you should go ahead and get the party started!

March 22:
GOOD MORNING! With all the stress in our society right now, some people are having a hard time dealing with situations they may be facing. We never know what some may be facing behind closed doors. If you see, or know, of someone who seems to be "distant"; please talk to them. Let them know you care. Let them know they are important to you. Do not wait until later and find out it was too late to have a conversation. Enjoy your day and your

time with your loved ones. May you be blessed and may something unexpected and positive come your way! Get the party started!

March 23:
GOOD MORNING! What a great day to be alive! Easter week celebrates the death of Christ. His death is a celebration because his life was given so the sins of man can be forgiven. It does not matter what you have done. He will forgive you of all your sins and/or all of your wrongs; if you just ask. This is why the difference in those who are afraid to die and those who are not afraid. The beginning of Easter week is celebrated by Christians, as Palm Sunday, or the day Jesus entered Jerusalem. Everyday brings you a little closer to the end of your time here. Christians are at peace with leaving this world. Many non believers are not. God knows you. Do not wait until it is too late to speak to him. He wants to hear from you. Plan on attending a church service this Easter. It could be a service on a media site. Talk to God. You can do it anywhere at anytime. He is always there. May this be a blessed day for you and your loved ones!
Enjoy this day!

March 24:
GOOD MORNING! May this be a great day for you and your loved ones! May you be blessed with good health, wisdom and guidance. Treat others as you would like to be treated. Be selective of your "friends." Let those you are close to, know you care and help others when you can. Life is short. Be active and leave the negative in the past. Keep positive thoughts in your mind. Do not expect more than you are willing to give. Enjoy this day and make the best of every minute. Today is a gift. Get your party started!

March 25:
GOOD MORNING! Welcome to the first day of the rest of your life. Challenges are coming at people from many different directions these days. It may be financial, medical, personal or business. It seems like dealing with turmoil and chaos is a constant for many. People are under stress and they project it in everything they do. People need to have more patience and not get pulled into other's chaos or issues. At the same time, try not to be judgmental. Unless you know what others may be going through and have been there; you cannot appreciate the stress they may have. There are a lot who are hurting these days. A little extra patience may save a

relationship or keep someone from a lifetime of regrets. Keep moving forward and be thankful for what you have and who you are. Help others when you can. One day it could be you who needs the help. Enjoy your day! Go ahead and get your party started!

March 26:
GOOD MORNING! May this day be a blessed day for you and your loved ones. May you be blessed with good health, wisdom, patience and guidance. Do not believe everything you are told or hear. If you listen closely to what people say, you may find what they say and what they mean are two different things. Trust in yourself. If something does not sound right or does not feel right then it probably is not right. Today is your day and it can be a great day. Let it be that way. Leave the drama behind and move on with the positive. Enjoy this day and go ahead get your party started!

March 27:
GOOD MORNING! How about if you make this a special day? Do something really good for yourself today. Do something that you might not normally do. Go sit in a park, by a lake or maybe even in the woods. Listen to the wind and leaves, feel the cold in the air or maybe the sun on your face. Listen to the birds. You may even want to do this with someone special. May the appreciation for what is around you, be with you all day. Spread your smile and joy with others you come across. Speak to those you pass and always be in the positive. Enjoy this day. It is a gift from God. Make it count!

March 28:
GOOD MORNING! What a great day this is to be! Do you feel that? That is the blessing of life you have been given today. It is wonderful. No matter what is going on in your life, it is up to you how the day is going to be. Spend part of your day doing something good for someone else. A great gift is one which no one knows who gave it and cannot be paid back. Appreciate what you have and share it. If you are happy and poor you have more than the person with millions and is unhappy. Make the most of every minute and thank God for this day. It is truly a gift and deserves to be made the best you can. Go ahead and get the party started!

March 29:

GOOD MORNING! Welcome to your newest day! So glad you are here! Yesterday was the day symbolized as the day Jesus was crucified. Sunday represents the day he rose. As we go into the last couple of days of the Easter celebration, I am hoping many will take a few minutes and think about what all this celebration is about. Today will be one day closer to end of your life in this world. Have you thought about the next life? If you have not, this may be a good time. When you die, you are going to one of two places. Some may think this is funny. I am hoping you know there is a another world after this one. May this be a truly great day for you! Be blessed with good health and a smile and a word for others. Enjoy this day!

March 30:

GOOD MORNING! May this new day be a blessing to you and your loved ones. The celebration of the crucifixion of Christ is one of the two most important celebrations of the Christian faith. Please take the time to reflect upon the celebration of this time. Take the time to have a prayer today and thank God for giving the life of his son for you. There will come a day when you may be face to face with God. You may want to let him know you believe now. Tomorrow may be too late. Make this a special day for your children so their memories can be shared with their children. Attend a church which celebrates this time in history. If you cannot find your way to the car maybe a sermon via a media will work for you. May this be a great day for you and your loved ones. Enjoy this day as special as it is!

April 1:
GOOD MORNING! It is a great day to be alive. Welcome to the newest day of your life. May you be blessed with wisdom, good health and a heart filled with happiness. Do not expect anything if you do not do anything. Be active in your life and your life will be exciting. An active day will also bring a feeling of accomplishment; which will give you a feeling of value. A feeling of value will give happiness. That you can share with others. You get what you give in this life. Give a lot and you can expect a lot. Enjoy this day and make the best of every minute. It's your day!

April 2:
GOOD MORNING! There are some days when things are just going to be tough. People may be getting their last paycheck, bad report from a doctor or a death in the family. It would be extremely difficult to not feel pain on some days. If people did not have days like this, they would not know some of the emotions these situations bring. Without knowing the tough times, it is harder to appreciate the great times. Try to remember even on the worse of days the end of the day will come. Tomorrow you will have more knowledge and may have learned a valuable lesson. Make the best of the bad situations and keep moving forward. Do not dwell on the bad times. God never gives more than you can handle. Make the best of this day. It is a gift. Go ahead and get the party started. It's yours...

April 3:
GOOD MORNING! It is a new day and this is where your new life begins. It is a fresh start and nothing from yesterday can hold you back. Let go of your fears and move forward. You can accomplish anything you want, if and when you put your mind and heart to it. Make this a day you'll remember for yourself and others. Do something special. Whether it be small or big, leave a positive memory. Others learn from you and you from others. Enjoy this day and appreciate the gift it is. Get the party started! It's yours!

April 4:
GOOD MORNING! It is so good to see you today. There is someone who needs you today. They may just need to see you or maybe they need to hear your voice. They may need to share something with you and are seeking your advice. You are loved and you are needed. You may not be told this everyday. You have to know you

are special and you are here for a positive reason. There is a lot of negative behavior in the world these days. Please do not allow the negative people to negativity effect your life. Keep your eyes open and believe in the actions rather than words. Do not let others hold you back. May you be blessed. You have the ability to do almost anything. God loves you and he would like to hear from you today! Go ahead and get your party started!

April 5:
GOOD MORNING! Isn't it great to be here today? It is a great day to be alive. Appreciate the people in your life. Many of the people you will come into contact with will effect you in some way. A chance and brief encounter may effect you for the rest of your life. A five minute conversation may inspire you years later or carry with you forever.   You will learn something from everyone. It is up to you what you learn, how much you will use in your life and how you will use what you learn. Never feel a conversation is a waste of time. Could be the biggest mistake of your life. Enjoy this day and share your joy and happiness with others. There is so much to be grateful for. Go ahead and enjoy this day. It is yours so make the best of it!

April 6:
GOOD MORNING! Thank God you have been given a new day! It is truly the first day of the rest of your life. Everyday is a gift, no matter what is going on in your life. You have been given a chance to make it good for yourself. You also have the ability to share, something good, with others. It is an opportunity to make a difference in someone else's life. There are people who need you and look to you; whether, you know it or not. Speak kindly with, and have patience with, others. Many do not want to ask or hesitate to ask for help. Others may just want your conversation. Your presence may be all the comfort someone needs. It may be you who needs help one day. Have a blessed day and may you and your loved ones be healthy and protected from harm. Enjoy this day. It is your party!

April 7:
GOOD MORNING! Life is so short and there are so many things to enjoy while we are here. Getting older, may bring about a change in our priorities and what is important. Unfortunately, sometimes

it takes a tragedy to show many what is really important in life. Terminal illnesses can have that effect. A major traffic accident without warning can be life altering. No one will escape passing from this world. Do not wait until a person, who is important to you, passes away or finds out they have a terminal illness, to visit or contact. Take some time away from your busy schedule and contact others who might have been an inspiration or effected your life in some way. Maybe it's a family member or a distant relative you have not seen or talked to in many years. It may even be someone you spoke to only once but that conversation or meeting stuck with you. In the end it will be your health and loved ones who are the high priorities of our lives. Live without regrets think about your priorities in life. Tomorrow may be too late. Enjoy this day. It is a gift from God!

April 8:
GOOD MORNING! It is a great day to be alive. Today is a great day to forgive all who have wronged you or your loved ones and move forward with your life. Let go of all the negative feelings you have. Fill that new space with positive energy and grow in your strength in all ways. Focus on what abilities God has given you and not what you wish you had. Positive attitude can make all the difference in your life. Wealth is not all about money. You can be rich in spirit, character, generosity, knowledge and so many other things. Use your abilities and have faith in your self! God has given you what you need. Make the best of this day and go get it!

April 9:
GOOD MORNING! Today is a great day to turn your back on the problems of yesterday. Deal with the issues you have and move on. You have been blessed with your own mind to do your own thinking. No one person knows everything. No one person can deal with everything. Smart people will ask for advice or seek guidance. It is important to put serious consideration to who you seek guidance from. Unless a person has been through what you are going through they cannot possibly understand how you are feeling. Unless someone has been in a situation like you are in, their advice may not have the experience you need. Praying may give you the help you need. Whatever you may be facing, the sun will still come up tomorrow. Make the best of every minute today and enjoy this day as the gift it is. Go ahead and get the party started!

April 10:
GOOD MORNING! Time to get the day started. Let's get the coffee down, teeth brushed, and the peeper's open. Time is wasting. The sun is up and it is time to make things happen. Do not wait for things to come to you. You need to go get it. Please, be kind and speak to those you pass. Make new friends today. Do something special for someone. Appreciate what you have and share what you have with others. Go ahead and get this day started. It's your party! Make it count!

April 11:
GOOD MORNING! Don't just talk about what you want to get done. Take control of your day. Make positive things happen today. Keep your attitude positive and drop the negative from your thoughts. Not only will your day feel like it is better, it will be better. Share some of those positive feelings with others. You just never know what some kind words might mean to another. Enjoy this day and all it brings. It is a gift so maybe you can get that party started now!

April 12:
GOOD MORNING! No matter what you feel like today, feel blessed to be here. Many may see the day begin and not see it end. Many will lose a loved one today. Many have a limited time here and they know it. Everyday you wake up is a blessing, no matter what is going on in your life. Be appreciative of your time and make the best of every minute. You are not guaranteed the next. May this be the greatest day of your life. Do something special for someone else and speak to those you pass. Enjoy your day!

April 13:
GOOD MORNING! May this be a great day for you and your loved ones. May you make a difference in your life and leave a positive memory in your wake. To quote a portion or a sermon I recently heard, "if money is all you leave when you die, you have not left much." Think big and make your actions bigger. May you and your loved ones be blessed with good health, wisdom, guidance and success. Enjoy this day as the gift it is. Go ahead and get your party started!

April 14:
GOOD MORNING! Just make this a great day. Try not to complain today. Try to eliminate any negative comments from your conversation. You may be amazed at how, being positive, makes you feel. Life is good. What makes it better is what you make of it. Speak to those you pass and let others know you care. Learn from others and trust in God. Get this day started and share it with someone special. Go ahead and get the party started!

April 15:
GOOD MORNING! Looks like you have been blessed with a new day. You need to get it moving. You are here for a reason and you have a purpose; whether, you know it or not. Live your life to it's fullest. Make the best of this day and everyday. Make your life count for something good. Be slow to anger and patient with others. Let your loved ones know you care. Make this a great day and make it count for yourself and others. Get your party started!

April 16:
GOOD MORNING! Here is hoping you were able to sleep well last night, are rested and refreshed for a new day. Here is also hoping you will take a moment and have a little talk with God before you leave your home, or go out the door, this morning. There are people who will not be able to go out their door any longer. They were perfectly fine and healthy yesterday. Their purpose had come to an end and they were taken from this world. Their lives changed in a blink of an eye. If you have a doubt about Heaven and Hell, just go to the internet and you will find people who have been to both. Books have been written in great detail about the trips others have taken and then returned to this world. Hell, is not a place you want to go. Some do not believe in Jesus Christ and God. Usually, you can tell by their actions, or lack of actions. It is not they are "bad" people. They just do not have the faith. Some may be angry with God. Please, speak to him today. You can talk to him anytime. He is there all the time and he is wanting to hear from you. Isn't it better to believe in God and find out he does not exist; then to not believe and find out he does? He may be the piece of life you have always felt was missing. He can bring peace to a troubled heart and mind. May you all, along with your loved ones, be blessed today. May you be given wisdom and good health. May you also be blessed with peace in your life. Cherish your time with your loved ones. Let them know you love them. You just never know when

your purpose here may be done. Enjoy this day! Go ahead and get the party started! Today is a gift!

April 17:
GOOD MORNING! It's a new day and the start of your new life. It is up to you what you make of it. You are loved and needed by others. It may not always feel like it; however, you are important to others. You are loved for the person are, not a person you could be. Be yourself and be happy in who you are. God made us all different for a reason. There is something special about everyone, including yourself. If and when you learn what special talent you have been blessed with, it may provide you with insight into what you can really accomplish, in this world. Be blessed and have faith in yourself. May this be the greatest day of your life!

April 18:
GOOD MORNING! Doesn't it feel good to be alive? As long as you are going to be in the world today, you may as well make it the best day you have ever had. Do not let others pull you down. Use only positive thoughts and speech. Change those "I do not think I can" to "I will see what I can do." Say, "hello" to those you pass and get to know others. Be grateful for this day and the time you have here. Make the best of every minute. Go ahead and get your party started!

April 19:
GOOD MORNING! Welcome to the newest day of your life! This may be a great day to talk, visit or reach out to family members or loved ones you have not connected with lately. Lives change in the blink of an eye. Many people forget how short life really is. Many do not have an appreciation for it until later in their lives. A stroke, an automobile accident, plane crash, or a quick trip to the store can change everything in a moment. You may be faced with apologizing to someone for harsh words; when they may never be able to say, "you are forgiven." You may be faced with the memory of your last words to a loved one being unkind. This is not a good thing to have to have live with. Don't let this happen to you or your loved ones. Never leave your home angry and never go to bed angry. Make peace with others. Is it so important who is right and who is wrong? Sometimes there only opinions and no clear right or wrong. No one knows how their lives may be effected today. Make the best of every minute and let those you love, know you

care. Enjoy this day and appreciate the gift it is. Go ahead and get your party started!

April 20:
GOOD MORNING! It's a new day. It has been given to you as a gift. You can make it as good as you want it to be. No matter what comes your way today; keep in mind what a great gift you have been given; the gift of life. If you keep in mind how great this gift is and where it comes from all your issues will seem smaller. Not everyone will have the appreciation for life you do. Those without appreciation are the people which issues seem to come from. Those without an appreciation are who make decisions without guidance or wisdom. They feel they are smarter than everyone and do not look to God because they know more than others. Most have alternative motives for their decisions and their decisions often do not make sense. Do not allow yourself to be pulled into their world. We all pay for our actions. Sooner or later, those who create chaos in this world will suffer for their decisions. Some will continue that type of life until they die and some will ask for to be forgiven. Appreciate what you have been given and work towards what you would like to have. Make the best of everyday. Enjoy it all. Go ahead and get your party started!

April 21:
GOOD MORNING! So good to see you today. Your presence has already made this a special day. May you be blessed with good health, wisdom and guidance today. May your heart be filled with the peace and joy you were meant to have. Smile and speak to those you pass. Laugh often and enjoy life. Let go of your worries. Make the best of every minute of the day and share your happiness with your loved ones. Enjoy your life!

April 22:
GOOD MORNING! Congratulations on the newest day of your life! People will come and go in your life. Most will be acquaintances; few will be true friends. The true friends are special people and everyone has them. You may not see them often. You may be separated by distance. Your activities may keep you apart. They are always there for you and you for them. They are the ones you can call for advice. They are the ones who will always tell you the truth. They will protect your name and defend your character, if need be. Their opinion of you is the same; whether, you are present, or not.

Choose carefully who you call friend. They are as important as your family. Make this a great day for yourself and others. Smile and speak to those you pass. Help others when you can. May you be blessed and share your blessings with others. Go ahead and get the party started. This day is a gift!

April 22:
GOOD MORNING! Hope you slept well and feel good today. The day has started and it is moving on. It needs your involvement. There is someone looking for you to touch their life today. You are needed and your presence is needed. Maybe today is the day you can do something really special for someone. It does not have to be money or a face to face situation. Someone may just need to hear your voice. Someone may need some clothes you do not wear any longer. There is nothing like letting others know you care. Hugs work wonders and are just what many need. They are free and do not take much from you or your schedule. Today may be someone else's day, tomorrow it may be you in need. Take advantage of this time and make it count for someone else, as well as yourself. Doing for others always gives a good feeling. Enjoy this day and make the best of every minute. Take a moment and thank God for being able to help others.

April 23:
GOOD MORNING! Time to get the body moving into the flow of this new day. Get your coffee, tea, juice or whatever drink that may start your day and get those teethies brushed and get those peepers open. Just waking up is a great way to start the day. Try a healthy breakfast, do a little dance and get this day started. Leave your loved ones with kind words, say a little prayer for guidance and wisdom and move out into the world. May it be a great day for you! May this be the greatest day of your life. Make the best of every minute and go get it! This day is yours and for you!

April 24:
GOOD MORNING! Oh Happy Day! You are here! Take a deep breath. Can you smell that? That is the smell of the start the newest day of your life. Smells good, doesn't it? Whatever yesterday smelled like, is gone, over, goodbye, no more. Let it go and focus on the sweet scent of this new day. The more you look forward to it, the better it will smell. Everyone should be looking forward to their day. You are special to someone and are needed. It may not

always seem like it, or feel like it. God has a plan for you. Hope you learn what that plan is...Enjoy this day!

April 25:
GOOD MORNING! It is a new day and so glad you are here to enjoy it. Today is the day to change anything in your life you do not like and the day to thank God for the things you do like. Keep in mind, who you are happens to be a combination of all of your past; whether, you like it or not. You are special and there is a special purpose for you to be in this world. Every negative action in your life also has a positive action. If you are truly a Christian and believe in Jesus Christ, you have someone to turn to in the hard times. If you do not Know Christ or God, then it may be a good time to have a talk with him. You do not have to be on your hand and knees. You can talk to him anywhere at anytime. Make this a special day for yourself and those you love. Be at peace and let go of the turmoil or drama in your life. Spend your time on the positive. Get your day started. Someone is waiting on you!

April 26:
GOOD MORNING! Today is special, now that you are here. During your lifetime there will be special people who cross into your life. Some of these encounters may be just a few minutes; however, that brief time may stick in your mind forever. Some of these people may always be a part of your life. There is just no limits to what you may learn from others. You have to be willing to listen to others to learn. Make this a great day for your self and your loved ones. It is a special day with you here. Let your loved ones know you care, Enjoy this day like no other. May you and your loved ones be blessed! It is your day. Go get it!

April 27:
GOOD MORNING! Today is your day. God has given you this day because your job is not done here. If you have not found your purpose in this world today may be the day you find it. May there be peace in your life. May your heart be filled with the joy it was meant to have. May calm and patience be with you throughout your day. May you be able to touch the lives of others with a smile, kindness and generosity. Lift you head high. You are unique, loved and special. Be yourself. You are as special as they come. Make this day count!

April 28:
GOOD MORNING! Once you get those peepers open this morning take a little time to step outside and feel the fresh air. Take a deep breath and let your lungs fill with the start of your new day. It is a great day to be alive and I am so glad you are here. Call someone special and be the first to wish them a GOOD MORNING. Let them know how much you care about them with a "thank you" for being a part of your life. Let this be a great day for yourself. Ignore the negative and laugh at your mistakes. Appreciate what you have and share what you can. May this be the greatest day of your life. Go ahead and get your party started. Everyday life is a little shorter. Make it count!!

April 29:
GOOD MORNING! When your little peepers open and your mind clears today; just know how blessed you are. There are families who will wake up today and be less one family member or loved one. Take a moment and thank God for being here today and having those you love in your life and in your day. Tomorrow may be a different story. Do not take your day for granted. Make the most of every minute!

April 30:
GOOD MORNING! Today is a great day to look around and appreciate the blessings you have been given in this life. For every negative occurrence there is something positive to be gained or learned. Even the survivor of cancer has been blessed. It is all about how you look at the situation. Being blessed is not always about the material things. It could be a job you really enjoy. It could be something you have done for someone; which, really gives you a special joy. It could be a person in your life, or a place you have been which is special to you. Blessings are represented by different things to different people. Be happy in this day. Share your joy with others and get this day started. It is a gift. Now get moving and get your party started!

May 1:
GOOD MORNING: May this be a great day for you and your loved ones. May you and your family be blessed with good health. May you be blessed with wisdom for your decisions. May you have direction and the best of guidance. May your heart be filled with the joy it was meant to have. May you have peace in your life. Know you are loved. Know you are special and needed in this world. Go on out there and leave your mark in this world. Leave positive thoughts wherever you go. Enjoy this day and be glad in it!

May 2:
GOOD MORNING! It would be great if we could back up and relive our lives a second time and maybe correct our wrong choices and decisions. Unfortunately, that is not the case. We get one chance to live our lives and need to make the best of life the first time around. Think about how much you could get accomplished if all the negative thoughts were removed from your mind. Nothing would be holding you back. Maybe you can just let go of the negative thoughts and feelings you have and at the same time fill that space with positive thoughts. Try and go one day without any negative comments, or thoughts towards others. See how much better you will feel. May this be the very best day of your life. May something special come your way today and may you be able to share it with others. Smile and speak to those you pass. Your life is short. Never let an opportunity pass which you can help another. Enjoy this day and all it has to offer! Go ahead and get this party started!

May 3:
GOOD MORNING! Welcome to your newest day. It is the first day of the rest of your life. Through genetics, diet and lifestyle, personal health quality is different for everyone. It is by the Grace of God some are healthy and some have medical issues. Keep this in mind when you have an opportunity to help someone who may not be as healthy as you. Many are not able to pay for their medications and food, or medications and utilities. There are so many in need. It only takes an illness, or an accident, to put you in a situation where you need the help. Don't wait for someone to ask for help. If you see a need, step forward. It makes you feel good to do something special for another. Enjoy this day and be safe in it. You have been blessed. Share it with others!

May 4:

GOOD MORNING! It appears you have been blessed with a new day. Life is such a gift and should be appreciated as just that, a gift. Some feel it is all about what life can give them. Others feel it is more about what they can give and how they can help others. In the Christian faith, it is believed we are here because God allowed his son to die for others. Giving your life for others is more than most will ever be asked to do. If you were asked to do that, would you? Many, would not hesitate. Since, that is probably not going to be asked of you today, maybe you could still give something of value. Maybe just a little portion of your time. Give some time to your loved ones. Give some time to those you may not know and have no one else in their lives. Maybe, it is someone you pass on the streets. Maybe, it is someone in a nursing home. Give some thought and prayer to those who have been important to you in the past. Most importantly, give some time to God. Have a moment of prayer sometime today. It could be the most important time you ever spent. Enjoy this gift of a day. Live life to it's fullest. Do not leave any regrets in your path. Go ahead and get the party started! It's your new day!

MAY 5:

GOOD MORNING! It is so good to see you here today. There are people waiting and expecting to see you today. You may not even know who is looking forward to seeing you. It may be someone you would not expect. You are important to others. You are loved and you have a purpose in this world. Your purpose may change the life of someone for the better. Your purpose may be the inspiration someone else needs to pick themselves up and move forward in their life. Thank you for being here and welcome to the first day of the rest of your life! Be at peace with yourself and those around you. Let your loved ones know you care and love them. You make this day better! Thank you.

MAY 6:

GOOD MORNING: It's a new day and it is a gift to you. Appreciate the gift of every new day and make them the best you can. You only get one chance per day. Tomorrow is never a guarantee. Take care of your loved ones when you are here and while you can. Help others when you can. Let others know you care about. Make this a great day for yourself and others. You are here to be happy, successful and compassionate to others. You may want to take the time to Thank God for this day and all it will bring. Go ahead and get your party started!

May 7:
GOOD MORNING! What a great day it will be today. No matter what you have going on in your life; there is someone who would gladly trade their life for yours. Before you complain about having trouble seeing; consider there are those who have never seen. Before you complain about being overweight, consider those who have no food. Before you complain about being too hot; consider those who have no shelter. Appreciate what you have been given. We are all different. Use what God has given you. We all are given special talents and abilities in our lives. It is up to you what you do with them. God does have a plan for you; whether you believe in him or not. Make a difference in someone's life today. It may just take a smile or a brief few minutes of your life. Make the most of every minute of your day. Every minute is a blessing! Treat them as the gift they are. No matter what you are facing someone is facing something worse. Go ahead and get your party started. People are waiting are on you!

May 8:
GOOD MORNING! Time to start making things happen. There are things to do and people to see. Let your motivation be guided by your enthusiasm to succeed and your faith in yourself! Do not listen to anyone telling you "it cannot be done." Be persistent and be active. Things do not get better by doing the same thing over and over the same way. New things need new approaches. There is no such thing as failure. There are temporary setbacks. Go ahead and get this day started. It is yours to make it what you want it to be! Get your party started! You are loved and needed..

May 9:
GOOD MORNING! Today is a great day to let go of any fears you may have. Fear comes from the unknown and uncertainty. Probably the most powerful fear, is the fear of rejection. No one should carry the fear of rejection. We are not going to be liked by everyone and that is alright. You are not going to like everyone either. The fear of being ridiculed by another or others is a big fear. No one is perfect. No one is better than anyone else in this world. Everyone is special in some way. The fear of failure is tremendous in some people. The only failure is not trying something new or a

different way. No matter what the outcome of trying something new, you will be one step closer to success. Dying is another fear many have. If you have a true faith in God, you will not be afraid to die. Let go of your fears today. They can hold you back from success. They can hold you back from completing your life. If you have faith in God, you have no limits. Make this day count. Go ahead and get your day started and do not look back. It is a gift and it is your day. Go ahead and get your party started!

May 10:
GOOD MORNING! May today be the greatest day of your life. May your thoughts be all positive and your day productive. May your heart be filled with the joy God's children were meant to have. Meet others with a smile and speak with kind words. . Share your happiness with others. May you be blessed with wisdom and guidance. Help someone today. May this be a blessed day for you and your loved ones. This day is a gift. Make the best of every minute. Go ahead and get your party started!

May 11:
GOOD MORNING! Everyday you wake up is a special day. God has blessed you already. So good to see you here. Today is a day you can share with others in happiness, love, joy, and faith. Be the person you were meant to be. You were made as you are for a reason. Trying to be someone else will not give you happiness. Be happy in yourself. God made you special for a reason. Do not rush things in your life. They will come in God's time. You are special. Enjoy this day and all it brings! It is a gift for you!

May 12:
GOOD MORNING! It is a new day! It is wonderful to wake up, clear the eyes out, maybe get the coffee, tea or juice flowing then stick your head outside and feel the fresh air in your lungs and hear the birds waking up too. Life is good. It may not always be easy. Some have more hurdles than others. Life just seems to get better as we go; if you are looking at it through clear eyes with a clear head. Today may be the day you meet a special someone who will be your friend for life. Today may be the day you help someone who will always remember you for an act of kindness you showed them. Today may be the day you do something or say something your children or loved ones will always be grateful for. Of course, nothing will happen unless you get moving and get the

day started. Go ahead and get this day moving and enjoy every bit of it. No matter what this day it is a blessing! May this be the best day of your life!

May 15:
GOOD MORNING! This is a great day to share your smile with others. Just a smile and quick "hello" may be all someone needs to hear from another person to completely change their day for the better. There may be some days you may not feel like smiling. It may help to remind yourself of all the blessings you have been given. Think of the places you have been, things you done, people you have met or your loved ones. Material things do not give people happiness for a lifetime. It is the things you cannot put a price on that seem to be most important and bring the most happiness. How many people would give everything they own for some time with a loved one who has passed? Keep others in your mind as you go through the day. Help when you can. Many are hurting whether: physically, financially, and/ or mentally. Remember, sometimes, it just takes a smile. Let your loved ones know you love them, before you lose that ability. May today be the greatest day of your life!

May 16:
GOOD MORNING! Welcome to your newest day. As you stretch and yawn and begin your wake up routine, consider having a little word of prayer for yourself, your loved ones and those around you. The Bible tells us to pray for our leaders. (they really do need the help) Many are needing help these days and prayer may be the only relief some can find. Prayer may also be the only avenue left to many. God knows who you are. He is waiting to hear from you. You may want to talk with him, while you still have time here. He may give you peace you have never known. Treat others as you would want them to treat you. Smile and speak to those you pass. May your heart be filled with the joy it was meant to have. Go ahead and get the first day of the rest of your life started. It is truly a gift and may you and your loved ones be blessed with good health, wisdom and guidance! Get your party started!

May 17:
GOOD MORNING! Congratulations, you have been given another day. Today is the day you can make use of all the lessons of the past. No one is perfect. You are not expected to be perfect and you

should not expect others to be perfect. Learn from your mistakes. Mistakes are lessons of life. Life does not change for those who do the same thing, the same way, everyday. Change your life. If you do not talk to God, today may be a good day to start. You can do that anywhere at anytime. Do not put it off until it is too late. Enjoy this day and all it brings. May you and your loved ones be blessed. It is your party, get it started!

MAY 18:
GOOD MORNING! It is a great day to be alive. Our bodies are such miracles. Life is such a miracle. Sometimes people forget just how fragile and what a miracle life is. Just the simple act of sitting up is such an orchestrated accomplishment of nerves, thought processes, blood and air flow, muscle and bone coordination. Your body is truly a miracle. Everyone should have an appreciation for what miracles, they, and their bodies are. When you think about that miracle, it makes all the negative from others seem so small, petty and minute. Let go of the negatives in your life. Try to figure out what your purpose is and put your energy to work there. You will be much happier and your life will be so much more fulfilling. Take the time to know others. Speak to those you pass. Help others when you can. Enjoy this gift of a day. This is your day. Make the best of every minute!

May, 19:
GOOD MORNING! Let's make this a great day for everyone you come into contact with. Smile and speak to those you pass. Take the time to know the person in line with you. Be patient with the people who make mistakes. (maybe they'll be patient with you) Help those you can. Listen to those who need to release some emotions. Let your loved ones know you care. Never leave anyone when you are angry. Have a prayer before you leave home and treat others as you would want them to treat you. It is a new day for you. Make the most of every minute. Go ahead and get this day started!

May 20:
GOOD MORNING! Welcome to the newest day of your life. Tomorrow is never a guarantee. Whether it be a storm, natural death or an accident; someone you love or care about can be taken in the blink of an eye. Let those you love know it. Take the time to speak to those who mean a lot to you. We are here for only a short time.

Make the best of your time here. Be a good role model for your children. We will be moving into another life from here. For some it will be a good life. For some, there will be unimaginable suffering. Teach you children about God and his Son. It will be the most important thing you can do for your children. Take a moment and have a word with God. Let God know you know and believe in Him. One day you will call upon Him. Do not wait until He is needed to speak to him. He already knows you. Material things can be replaced, loved ones cannot. Keep in mind what is most important in this world.

May 21:

GOOD MORNING! Welcome to your new day. Sometimes when decisions need to be made, you might find there is not a right decision or wrong decision. You may want to call it the lesser of two evils or the decision with the least repercussions. You may not feel good about the decision. The situation may not come out as good as you anticipated. There may be more repercussions than you expected. Asking God for guidance is always a good way to start when these decisions need to be made. If there is time, seeking guidance from sources who may have been in that situation may help. A good question you may want to ask is, "Five or ten years from now, will this be a good reflection on my character?" Sometimes you just have to do the best you can; whether, right or wrong, accept the results, and move on. No matter what the results you will be wiser. Make this a great day for yourself. Let go of any anger or frustration which may be holding you back. Let go of any negative thoughts and fill the void with positive. Extend your hand to help others. May you be blessed with guidance and wisdom. May your heart be filled with the joy it was meant to have. It is your new day. Go ahead and get the party started!

May 22:

GOOD MORNING! Here's a prayer this day will bring about special blessings for you and your loved ones. May you be given wisdom, strength, and guidance for the decisions you will make today. May you have peace in your heart. May your heart have the joy it was meant to have. May you live without fear. May you positively influence someone's life today. May you travel safely and may your health be good. May all your negative thoughts and feelings be replaced with positive. Make this day great no matter what comes your way. Remember there is always someone willing to be in your shoes any day of the week. Enjoy this day. It is a gift. Go ahead and get your party started!

May 23:
GOOD MORNING! Here is a new day to enjoy and spend with your loved ones. Start you day with a little talk with God. You may want to ask God for protection for your loved ones. You may want to ask God for guidance for your decisions. You may want to thank God for what you have and what you have been given. It is good to remember everyday is a gift to be grateful for. It is also good to appreciate what you have and what you have been given. Keep in mind materials things can be replaced. It is the things which you cannot put a price on; which are the most important. Let your loved ones know you care about them. Talk to them, spend time with them, send a note or a gift. Do not let a day go by without speaking to God. If you do not believe in the Bible and/or the Christian faith; there are plenty of people out there who are willing to share their experiences in heaven or hell with others. Do not wait until it is too late. Life is short. Make the best of this day and all it offers. May this be the best day of your life!

May 24:
GOOD MORNING! It is a new day with all kinds of new situations, ideas and things waiting for you. After a little word of prayer just go on out there and make the best of every minute. Do not be intimidated by others, or obstacles. Do not be shy. See all there is to see in this wonderful world. Take a walk in the woods and notice all the life around you. Go to the highest point in your area and look to the horizon. This world is so full of life. Most of what is around us is good. Some is not so good and can inject poison into your life. Be selective about your company. You were meant to be productive and happy in this world. If you are not, then maybe you need to find your purpose or change something in your life. May this be the best of days for you. Know you are special and loved. You are also needed by others. Let others know you care about them. This day is a gift from God. Go ahead and get your party started!

May 25:
GOOD MORNING! It is so good to see you here today. You have already made this day special. This day amounts to a very brief period in your life. As short as this time may be; it is important that

this day count in a positive way. That is up to you. No matter what comes your way keep your attitude positive. No matter what your situation, there are people with a lot worse in their lives. Life may not be easy; however, it is good. Keep moving forward and keep smiling. Help others when you can and share your happiness with others. Be generous with your time and self as well as tangible items. Let this be the best day of your life. It is a gift and should be shared with others. May you and your loved ones be blessed. Go ahead and get your party started!

May 26:

GOOD MORNING! Today is a good day to appreciate the freedom you have to come and go as you do. You live in the strongest country in the world. You are able to turn on lights by the flick of a switch, not the lighting of a candle. You can walk to your kitchen and enjoy something cold from your refrigerator. Your water comes from a faucet and not a bucket or a container. Do not take the blessings you have for granted. When you do there is a chance you will lose them. We are truly a blessed country and have enjoyed God's blessings for several centuries now. This country received this blessing because we were founded on the Christian faith. Thank God today and the many who have given their lives for you to be where you are. Make this a great day for yourself and loved ones. May this be the best day of your life!

May 27:

GOOD MORNING! You are here to be a success and be productive in your life. You are also here to take care of yourself and others. Leaving something for others to remember you by, everyday, takes discipline. Your accomplishments are up to you. Being able to positively effect the life of one person a day would be a great thing. Speaking to others as you pass them, visiting others who cannot get out, listening to others, extending your help to people who cannot do for themselves are things you will be remembered positively for. Fill your life with positive rather than negative and you will be surprised at how it may positively effect your health, attitude, and your feelings about yourself. Do something special everyday and your life may begin to change. Enjoy this day and all it brings. What is not a success is a lesson. This day is yours. Go ahead and get your party started!

May 28:

GOOD MORNING! Welcome to the newest day of your life. Glad to see you are here. The best way to start your day is with a prayer thanking God for this day and what he has given you. We may not always get what we want when we want. That is because we are being protected. Sometimes what we want is not good for us. All the decisions we make will have consequences. Some will be positive and some of the consequences will not be good. Think about the consequences of your actions before you commit to the act. May this be a blessed day for you and your loved ones. May your prayers be answered, may you have God's protection and may this be a special day for you. Enjoy your day and do something special for someone else!

May 29:

GOOD MORNING! With so much chaos and stress going on in people's lives these days, it is very easy to let your emotions get the best of you. Please give careful consideration to your words, before reacting to the words of others. When people speak in anger, their words are usually designed to hurt others. When you consider that brief moment of time; when you might feel a slight vindication and compare it to your entire lifetime, that brief moment will feel miniscule. More than likely, you will also forget that moment, as time goes on. Use this day to spread the joy you were meant to have in your life. Help others when you can. Let go of the negative which you may be carrying. Fill the void with positive thoughts and energy. Your life and this day are a gift. You are special and loved. Trust your life to God. Go ahead and get your party started!

May 30:

GOOD MORNING! Welcome to the newest and first day of your new life. It is a great day to be here. There are people who may float through life with few issues for a while. There are people who have issues everyday. There are people who have issues on occasion. Sometimes these issues are because of actions of people, sometimes these actions are from circumstances beyond people's control. No matter what the issue, life goes on. If you want change, change the way you are doing things. No matter what your situation, do not give up in life. Life is too good! Enjoy this day and all it has to offer.

JUNE 1:
GOOD MORNING! So glad you are here today. Start your day with a prayer and appreciate what you have been given. There is no such thing as a bad day. Some are a little tougher than others. Make the best of every minute of every day. Live without regret and leave a good memory in your wake. It's your day and you are needed. Go get it!

JUNE 2:
GOOD MORNING! Wake up, it's a new day God has given you. This is another day to find the purpose in your life or continue to work on the reason you are here. Your "purpose" will effect at least one other person. It may be someone you do not know and it may be someone you have known all your life. Your "purpose" may also effect many. Somehow, in some way, your life will have a positive effect in another's life. I pray everyone will find the "purpose" in their life. Sadly, some will not. Some will go through life never knowing how wonderful life is and what true happiness is. Before you leave your loved ones today, let them know they are loved. Let them know you care. Help others when you can. Share your smile and your good feelings with others. Let this the happiest of days for yourself and your loved ones. It is a blessing to be here and you have to know, this day is a gift. Go ahead and get your party started. It is your life to enjoy and share!

June 3:
GOOD MORNING! It appears you have been blessed with a new day to enjoy your life and loved ones! Can you imagine what you might get accomplished if you only had positive thoughts every day of your life? Today is a great time to make that as much of a reality as possible. Let go of any negative thoughts which surface and keep all the positive. We are here to be happy, positive, helpful, kind, compassionate, and generous to others. Do not let anger over come you. Life is short. Walk with a smile and speak to those you pass. Start the day with a prayer. May you and your loved ones have a blessed day!

June 4:
GOOD MORNING! Isn't it great to have another day to enjoy? Being hurt by others is something everyone will experience at some time or another, in their lives. It is very important to forgive those who have done the hurting and move on in your life. Dwelling on

that hurt is wasting time on something negative and non productive in your life. Every minute you spend on that pain is time you are being hurt again. It is always best to forgive and move on as soon as possible. You do not have to forget or let it happen again. Just do not dwell on it. Make this day as positive as you possibly can. Smile and speak to those you pass. Learn from the hurdles you experience. May you be blessed with good health, wisdom and direction for your decisions. This day is a gift of God. Make the best of every minute. Go ahead and get your party started!

June 5:
GOOD MORNING! Oh it feels so good to roll out of bed, yawn and stretch. Yep, you have been blessed with a new day! May you be blessed with good health and success today also. May this be a great day for you and your loved ones. Be patient, let your heart be filled with the joy it was meant to have. Enjoy this day as the blessing it was meant to be!

June 6:
GOOD MORNING! Doesn't it feel good to wake up and welcome this new day? This could very well be the best day of your life. It is not going to be the best day unless you get up and make it the best. You have been blessed already today. Thank God for the day. Let those you love, know you care. Forgive those who hurt you. Speak to those you pass. Be patient with others. Accept others as they are. Everyone is blessed with special traits. Make this a great day for yourself, your loved ones and those you come into contact with. You are needed and loved. Enjoy this day as the blessing it is. Make the most of every minute. Let others share in your joy!

June 7:
GOOD MORNING! It is a great day to be alive. It is a wonderful feeling to be able to stand and fill your lungs with the first deep breath of air for the day. You have been given the gift of life today. Share the joy of this gift with others as you go through your day. Speak only kind words to others. Help those who need help. Listen to those who need someone to talk with. Be careful what you ask God for. Make sure what you ask for is what you really want. Be appreciative of what you have. May this be a blessed day for you and your loved ones. May this also be the best day of your life. Take in that first big breath and go get this gift of a day. It is time to get your party started.

June 8:
GOOD MORNING! A new day has arrived and you are going to be a part of it. Make this day special for yourself. Do something for yourself you will remember twenty years from now, or even better, a lifetime. We all remember situations we have been in during our lives. Others may not always remember those situations the same way you do. It is better to leave good memories in your wake. Let your loved ones know you care. Enjoy this day as the gift you have been given. Go through the day with a smile. Speak to those you pass and treat others as you would want to be treated. May this be the most blessed day of your life. Enjoy what you have been given and appreciate what you have. It's your day, go get it!

June 9:
GOOD MORNING! It's a new day and it is your day, just for you. This day is a gift from God. His intention is for you to be happy and successful. First, you must believe and trust in God. The decisions you make, to get you there, will be your decisions. The consequences which follow your decisions, are what will bring happiness and success. Those consequences may also bring unhappiness. You may want to have a word of prayer for the guidance and wisdom you may need today. Not all decisions are easy or obvious. Enjoy this day and all it brings. Make the best of all that comes your way. This day is moving on. Go ahead and get your party started!

June 10:
GOOD MORNING! It's a new day. It is the first day of the rest of your life. This is a good day to set your priorities and goals. The more important things in life tend to be the intangible. Family and loved ones are who will remember you. Your character is what will remain after you pass from this world. How are you going to be remembered? No one person can be an expert in everything. Even the smartest people look for guidance for their issues. No matter what comes your way, keep your faith, and look for the positive in every situation. This day is a gift. Go ahead and get your party started!

June 11:
GOOD MORNING! You have already made this day special by being here. From this point on, the day will only get better. No matter what comes your way, walk and talk with a smile. You have what many others would like to have. There is something special about you, God has blessed only you with. Be happy with what you have been given. Appreciate who you are. Share your happiness and joy with others. Help others when you have the opportunity. Let your loved ones know you care. This day is a gift. Make the most of every minute and be happy with this gift! Today is your party. Get it started!

June 12:
GOOD MORNING! Doesn't it feel good to be alive? Sometimes you may get so bogged down in negative events in your life you lose sight of the positive and bright spots or people around us. We are all blessed with being a little different. Trying to change people is not always healthy for anyone. Accepting people and their "differences" is the first step to any good and healthy relationship. You do not have to have to like the "differences"; however, acceptance can give you time to build a positive outlook and relationship. You also do not have to give up your life for someone who has destructive behavior. Do not get so involved in negative situations that you are prevented from seeing the stars in a clear dark sky. You are here to be happy, productive and successful. Carrying around negative feelings is like carrying a lead weight. Deal with what you can and ask God to take care of the rest. You will be a lot happier and so will everyone around you. May this be the best day of your life. You have been blessed with a new day. It is up to you how much you enjoy it. It's your gift. Go get it!

June 13:
GOOD MORNING! Looks like God has decided your job is this world is not over. Congratulations on being given another day to enjoy with your loved ones or just being the special person God made you. Today may be the day you find out what your purpose in being here is; if you do not know already. It may be to effect the life of one. It may be to effect the lives of hundreds, or maybe even thousands. Everything you do, will have a ripple effect in this world. Your actions may only effect one. Then again it could effect many. May this be a blessed day for you. May only good things come your way. May you be a positive influence on someone's life

today. Smile and speak only kind words. Help others when you can. Today is a gift. Live it to it's fullest and make every minute count! Tomorrow is not a guarantee!

June 14:
GOOD MORNING! May you get as good as you give today. May you be blessed with more than you have prayed for. May you carry a smile and share it with all you meet. Speak to those you pass. Being part of a conversation means you have to listen also. Sometimes it helps everyone just to listen to others. Help everyone you can. One day you will need some help. Enjoy this day as the gift it is. It is time to get the day moving. Make every minute as it may be your last. It is your party. Get your party stared!

June 15:
GOOD MORNING! It is a great day to be alive. You being here, and alive, already makes this day special. There are people who need you and want to hear from, or see you. Share your yourself with your loved ones and others today. Let everyone you feel close to, know you care. Let your words be kind. Let your face and actions show happiness. Be strong in who you are. God made you special. Leave special feelings wherever you go. It is your day. Go get it and make good things happen!

June 16:
GOOD MORNNG! Today may just be the best day of your life. You should know that you are special and you are loved. The unknown causes fear. Fear is one of the most damaging of emotions. Being afraid of what may happen, is allowing that emotion to control you. Welcome every experience as a lesson. You should come out the other side wiser and smarter. The experience, occasionally, may be tough. It will pass and you will be better afterwards. Take as much control of your life as possible, and turn the rest over to God. He is always with you. He will never give you more than you can deal with. This is your day and your life. Do not be afraid. Go get it and get it with a smile. Enjoy your day!

June 17:
GOOD MORNING! Congratulations on the arrival to the newest day of your life. You have already been blessed today. This day has been made special by you. Whether you have rain or sunshine there is just so much to enjoy in this life. Today may be a great day

to take a few minutes and sit and listen to the wind in the trees, the rain falling on the ground, smell the vegetation around you, feel the ground beneath your feet, feel the texture of plants, feel the sun or rain on your face, hear the birds and squirrels talking to each other. After you spend a few minutes doing this you may want to take a minute and have a prayer and thank God for all he has given you and all the blessings in your life. Know you are loved. Know also you are already special. God does not make mistakes. Be yourself. That is the person everyone loves. This day is a gift. Live it to your best!

June 18:
GOOD MORNING! Well, it is official. Your job in this world is not done. Welcome to the newest day of your life. Get your morning coffee, tea, water, juice or whatever the case may be, take a deep breath, say, "Hello" to your new day and all those guardian angels around you, brush those teeth, and thank God for being here another day. Everyone is made up differently. Everyone has different looks. Everyone has different personalities. Everyone has a different way of processing their thoughts. It would be impossible, with so many variables, for everyone to come to the same conclusion, in the same way. Being tolerant of others is important in this world, at this time. Chances are the decisions being made, in your life, on a day to day basis, will be forgotten by you and whoever else may be involved, in the future. Just because another does not think, or feel, the same way as you, does not make them a bad person. Others just have a different way of processing, or rationalizing their thoughts. Keep your emotions in perspective. Be tolerant. Of course, those who intentionally hurt others are in a different category. Enjoy this day. Do not let the tough decisions drag you down. Do what you have to do and move forward. You have this minute. Tomorrow is not a guarantee. I am glad you are here. May this be the best day of your life!

June 20:
GOOD MORNING! It's here; a new day for you. Feel that wonderful feeling as your body wakes up? Your vision gets better, your body takes in new bursts of oxygen, your muscles stretch and it feels so good. You may stumble around for a few minutes getting something to help bring your body to the wake up status. You may have a furry friend who is talking to you, jumping on you or rubbing against you. Waking up is such a blessing. Everyday is so spe-

cial. Be bold, step outside when it is still quiet. Listen to the birds and other sounds of nature. Life is good. There will be hurdles; however, they will all pass. Love your day and love yourself. Today is God's first gift to you, of the day. Enjoy it and make the most of every moment. It's your party, go ahead and get it started!

June 21:
GOOD MORNING! New days bring new challenges, new ideas, new friendships, new feelings. Be sure to let your loved ones know how much you love them today. Be an inspiration to others. Smile and speak to all you pass. Get to know others. Spend time with your loved ones doing something new and different. Others look to you for attention and love. Be generous with those emotions. Be happy in yourself. You are made special for a special reason. May this be the best day of your life. May you receive what you give. May you be protected from harm. Enjoy this day as it has been given. A gift to you.

June 22:
GOOD MORNING! Welcome to the newest day of your life! May this day be only a blessing to you. May God protect you and your loved ones from harm. May you only think positive thoughts. May you only speak positive words. May you be protected and given guidance for your decisions. Start your day with a prayer and thank God for what you have. May you know only peace today and success in your ventures. This is your day. Make the best of every minute. You get one chance at this day. Give it your best. Enjoy this day as the gift it is!

June 23:
GOOD MORNING! May today be a day of peace for you and your loved ones. May contentment find you and fill your heart to bring the joy we are all to have in our lives. Maybe you can share that joy with someone who may not have any peace. Help all those you can. Let go of any resentment you may be carrying. Be grateful for who you are and what you have. You are special and you are loved. Live without fear. Make this the greatest day of your life. It is up to you how this day will look tomorrow. Make it count for something good!

June 24:
GOOD MORNING! Thank you for being in this world today. Your presence makes the world so much better for others. Your presence is also important. People look to you for compassion, love, understanding, guidance, wisdom as well as friendship. Be yourself. That is the person others like and love. You do not have to be someone else and you should never try to change who you are, for someone else. If someone is wanting you to change; then that person probably should not be a part of your future. If you have qualities you want to improve on, that is ok. God made you the person you are. You can always improve on yourself. Your personal traits are unique to only you. He has a plan for you. Give plenty of thought to your decisions. Guidance is always good. Just be sure where you get your guidance from is a good place to look for it. Enjoy this day as the gift it is. Let your loved ones know you care. Let go of the negative in your life and fill the void with positive. This day is a gift and you should make the most of every minute! It's your party, get it started!

June 25:
GOOD MORNING! A new day has been given to you. Everyday is such a blessing. It gives many a new chance to appreciate situations, or people, in their lives. The happiest people are the ones who love themselves as well as family and others. They look forward to the next day and getting up every morning. They bounce through their days. Challenges are only a bump in the road for these people. They do what they can to resolve issues and move on. Nothing holds them back. Their family and loved ones are important parts of their lives. Their thoughts, words and directions are all on positive notes. Let today be the most blessed day for you and your loved ones. May you know what true happiness is. No one is going to make you happy. It comes from within yourself. May this be the happiest day of your life. Share it with others. Go ahead and get this day started. It is a gift!

June 26:
GOOD MORNING! Here is a new day coming at you. Just being here is a blessing. Being able to make this day great is a privilege and blessing. Your options are many. It can be a day you'll be proud to relive later with others. It could be a day you did something special for someone and no one knew. It could be a day wasted. It is up to you. Life is short. Make everyday count for

something. Tomorrow is not a guarantee. Make the best of the time you have. Whatever you do, do the best you can and do it because it makes you feel good!

June 27:
GOOD MORNING! It is going to be a great day. The most important part of the day has already come. You are awake and alive. The rest of what comes is just a bonus. No one is perfect in this world. Everyone makes mistakes. Mistakes do not make you a lesser person. They do make you smarter. A mistake should teach you a lesson. The lesson is not for punishment but for your future reference and knowledge. Do not beat yourself up when those mistakes come along. Learn from them and remember them. They are part of what makes you the wonderful person you are. Let others know you care. There is nothing like a "hug" to say I care. Never leave your home in anger. Today is the first gift God is giving you. Enjoy it and make the best of every minute! Your new day is waiting for you, now go get it!

June 28:
GOOD MORNING! I just want to send a prayer out this morning for everyone. May this be a blessed day for you. May the Lord smile upon and give His guidance to the doctors and nurses working to help others. May you and your loved ones be protected from harm. May those who are ill be strengthened. May you be given guidance for your decisions. May you be given strength and the opportunity to help others. May you be given patience, compassion and peace. May you live without fear. May your faith remain strong. May those who do not believe have their hearts and minds opened today. May our leaders look to God for guidance and decisions which need to be made. God will answer prayers. May this be the greatest day of your life!

June 29:
GOOD MORNING! How about if you just make this a great day for yourself and others? Let go of all the negative feelings you have. Forget about those who have treated you wrong. Forget about the bad things you have heard. Say a prayer, take a walk, enjoy the outdoors. Listen to the birds or maybe the wind in the trees. The early morning is such a different world from what most are use to. It is peaceful and you have not had a chance to absorb the negative things surrounding you. It is a great day to be alive and others are

waiting to see and/or hear from you. Share your smile with others. Extend your hand and help those you can. Life starts out good. It is up to you to make it better. This is already a special day. Do not waste it. Go get it and leave something you can be proud of! Get your party started!

June 30:

GOOD MORNING! Looks as thought you have been blessed with another day of life in this world. That means your job, or purpose, here, is not done. It means there is something special you are meant to achieve. It may be helping one person. It may be one word someone needs to hear from you; which may change their direction in life. It may be you will effect many. Be assured, your life is to have a positive impact of at least one person. Sometimes people forget how special they are. Sometimes they just do not realize how special they are. Some are never told how special they are. Make a difference in someone's life today. Let them know how special they are. Call them, tell them, drop a note or email to them. You are special and you can let others know they are special too. Smile and speak to those you pass. Speak kind words to others today. You can make a lasting impression on someone. Make it a good one. May this be a blessed day for you and may this be the best day of your life!

July 1:
GOOD MORNING! Respect is important in life. There are different versions of respect. Most are more concerned about having "self respect." You were born with "self respect." You have the right of "self respect" as a living being. People learn more about "self respect" as they mature. You have to respect and love yourself before others will respect you. The respect you have will be directly related to your behavior and character. Some people will make good decisions throughout their lives; while others, may not make such good decisions. Most, still deserve a certain amount of respect. Keep this in mind when dealing with others. Speak to others kindly and thoughtfully. Be honest with others, if you desire to keep your "self respect." A deceitful person loses respect. If you show others respect, others will show you respect. You were born with respect. It is up to you to keep it. May this be a blessed day for you. May everything go well and keep those who are having difficult times, in your prayers. May today be the best day of your life.

July 2:
GOOD MORNING! Welcome to the first day of the rest of your life. Today is a gift. Make the most of every minute. Make the day count for something positive. May this be a blessed day for you and your loved ones. May you be safe and protected from harm. This day is yours. Go get it and make good things happen!

July 3:
GOOD MORNING! Welcome to your newest day of your life. With patience, you can enjoy so much more in life. Do not be in a rush to get tomorrow. There are still plenty of good things for today. Every time you hear, every time you feel, every time you taste, every time you see, you are experiencing a blessing from God. Appreciating what you have and what you have been given, is important in this life. Sometimes, people forget just how good their lives are and all the good things about their lives. All you have to do is take a deep breath every morning when you wake up and look around. It should be very easy to see what a miracle life is. It is not about the material things. It is about life itself. Appreciate it. Enjoy the time you have. Tomorrow is not a guarantee. Live today like this is your last day. May this be the greatest day of your life. May your heart be filled with the joy you are meant to have. Today is a gift from God. Appreciate this gift.

July 4:

GOOD MORNING! You have already made this day special by being here. Are you thankful for being able to live in this country? Do you ever think you could have easily been born in another country and lived a completely different life? Who have you thanked for the gift for living in this country? Our servicemen and women have given their lives to keep us free and from being taken over by others. How did you actually, come to be here? Some may feel like they were just randomly created by an act of nature. Some may describe it as coincidence of natural forces. You are not a coincidence and you are not random. You were brought into this world by God and for a purpose. This country was created the same way; with purpose. The purpose of this country seems to have been the worship, promotion and spreading of the word of God. We have been a productive, successful and for the most part, a protected country, for centuries. That has changed in the last sixty years. We are slowly taking God from our lives and replacing him with humanism. Many children know nothing of God or Jesus. We took him out of our schools where our children learn. We are slowly allowing a few to remove him from any type of public mention. As Christians, we are already being persecuted for our faith, even in our own homes. We are also, slowly, replacing God's law with man's law. There is a price to pay for breaking man's law and there is a permanent price to pay for breaking God's law. Thank you again, for making this day special. Who are you going to thank for making you special? May this be a blessed day for you and your loved ones. May you be protected from harm and may your eyes be open. Enjoy this day as the gift it is! Now is a good time to get your party started!

July 5:

GOOD MORNING! So glad to see you have a new day. Keep you eyes forward, the past behind you and carry no anger, no vindictiveness, and no hate. This will be a great day for you. Seize the opportunity to help others, speak to those you pass and get to know others. Never turn your back on someone who needs help. Start your day with a prayer and be grateful for what you have. This day is a gift. Enjoy it as it was given. May this be the best day of your life. Make it your best, no matter what. It is up to you!

July 6:
GOOD MORNING! Hopefully, you slept well and are ready for a new day. A new day will bring new adventures. Some of these adventures will be good, some may not be what you want to deal with. Some will have to deal with the loss of a family member or a loved one. Losing someone is always tragic. Usually the loss is due to age, or an illness, and expected. Sometimes, the passing is a complete shock and unexpected. These are tougher because you do not have a chance to say goodbye. You never know when the words you speak, as you leave to go to the store, work, or even bed, may be the last words you speak to someone. Make those words good. Speak to those you pass. Take the time to get to know others. You may be surprised of what you can learn. May this be the greatest day of your life. May you be blessed and protected. Sometime today, set aside a little time and speak with God. He knows you already. Today is a gift from Him. Go ahead and get your party started!

July 7:
GOOD MORNING! Welcome to the first day of your life. This day is brought to you by God. He has decided your job, in this world, is not done. He will be with you all day. Your angels will also be with you. They are the ones who keep your car from starting right away, hide your keys when it is time to go, or maybe spill something on your clothes to keep you from leaving at the time you had planned. A minute or two delay is all it takes to keep you from being in that accident that happened just before you got there. Don't be angry when things do not go as planned. It was probably in your best interest. Just because you want something; does not mean it is something you should get, or need. May your heart be filled with the joy it was meant to have. May you find your "purpose" in life. May you be able to help someone else today. It's your day and your "gift." Appreciate it and make the most of every minute. May this be the best day of your life!

July 8:
GOOD MORNING! Glad to see you today. Breath deep, say a prayer and then get that body moving for the newest day in your life. There are no successes without failures. Sometimes you have to get through the bad ideas before you can get to the good ones. If it did not work the first time, try a different way. The important

thing is to continue trying. Make this, a day to remember. You can do anything you want, if you try. May something special, and good, come your way today. May you be blessed beyond your dreams. May this be the best day of your life. It is your day, make it as good as you want!

July 9:
GOOD MORNING! May you have the peace and joy you were meant to have in your heart. Do what you can for the issues you may be having and turn the rest over to God. Good people do not have to tell others how good they are. Their actions speak for them. May this be a blessed day for you and your loved ones. May all the day go well. May you have the opportunity to help others and use it. God has blessed you with a new day. Make it count for something good. Leave a good memory in your path. It is your day. Go get it!

July 10:
GOOD MORNING! The sun is rising in your world today, no matter how good, or bad, yesterday was. It is a new and a different day. Yesterday is in the past, behind you, gone. Have an appreciation for your life. There are many who would find living in your world much better than the world they are presently dealing with. There is a place and a purpose for you in this world. You will have an opportunity to do something special for someone, or maybe many people, at some time in your life. You will make a difference in another's life. Our actions effect others. Let your actions be on a positive note. You are very important in this world. You are loved and needed. Speak to those you pass. Get to know those you meet. Help others when you have the opportunity. A smile from you, or just a "hello", may change another's whole world today. May this be the best day of your life. May something very special come your way today. Look to God for guidance. It is your day. Go get it!

July 11:
GOOD MORNING! You were blessed in many ways for this world. You were given a brain for your own thinking and decision making. You were given a conscience for your morals and behavior. The conscience is like the voice of God speaking to you. If something is troubling you or your conscience is bothering you then it is like a warning sign you may be doing something you should not. It may also be telling you more action is needed. A person without a

conscience is truly a dangerous person. That is a person who believes they are never wrong and they live life by their own rules. A society without faith and without conscience would be a dangerous place to live. Listen to your conscience. If your heart is right with God, then your conscience will not fail you. Enjoy this day and all it offers. Smile and speak to those you pass. Get to know others. Show others you care. Before you leave your loved ones today, say a prayer, tell them "you love them" and give them a hug. It may be the the most important part of your day! Today, is the first gift God is giving today. Make the most of it and enjoy every minute. Get your party started!

July 12:
GOOD MORNING! Welcome to your newest day. Waking up everyday is like getting a new car everyday. You wake up and take in a breath of that brand new car smell. Both are something people look forward to with anticipation. You could even compare your day to driving a Volkswagen or a Mercedes. Some days you ride a little better than others. Both get you where you want to go. Let today be like a nice ride to somewhere special. Enjoy the sights and all the day has to offer. Stay out of the mud and rough areas. Make the drive count for something. Do not let the day be wasted. It is your trip. Plan it well!

July 13:
GOOD MORNING! So good to see you are going to be here today. Hope you slept well, are rested and ready to wrap your arms around this day and all it brings. The beginning of a great day should start with a prayer of thanks and a request for guidance. Whatever you do today, do your best. Stand firm on your principals. You were given a brain and common sense to be able to reason for yourself. Use your eyes and ears to gain knowledge. Do not let others lead you down the wrong path. Help those you have an opportunity to help. Speak to those you pass. Get to know others. It is a small world and you never know who you may be speaking to. Make this a day to remember and leave a good impression on someone else's day. Let other's know you care. Give a hug whenever possible. Enjoy this day and it all it offers. It is a gift. Go ahead and get your party started!

July 14:

GOOD MORNING! May this be the best day of your life. "Do unto others, as you would have others do unto you." May you receive as you give in this world. Before you move into the anger mode in a situation; think before you speak and consider; is it really worth being angry about and is being angry going to change the situation? Let the situation be a lesson and move on. Enjoy this day as the gift it was given. Let your heart be filled with the joy it was meant to have. It is your day. Go get it and make it count!

July 15:

GOOD MORNING! Welcome to the newest day of your life. Before you leave your home or get to much into the day let the others in your home know how much you care about them. You may also want to thank God for giving you this newest day to enjoy. You are here to be happy in your life and successful. Part of that, is being happy with yourself and at peace with those around you. Everyday will not be a good day so you need to spend your time on what is most beneficial. Trying to change others is not going to give the peace you want or need. You can only change your own way of thinking and/or behavior. Others can only change themselves. May this be the greatest day of your life. May something very special come your way. This day is a gift and should be treated like it is. Enjoy every minute and make the best of it. Share your smile with others. Share your time with others. Never pass an opportunity to help others. It is your day, go get it!

July 16:

GOOD MORNING! Congratulations on your new day and all it will bring. Be grateful for this day. Be grateful for your family and/or loved ones. Be grateful for those around you. Be grateful for every breath you take. Before complaining about something or someone think of the parent who has just learned their baby has a rare disease and is not expected to live. Think of the parent whose child has just passed away unexpectedly and they were not able to say, "Goodbye." Think of the parent whose child has disappeared. Without a closure they will live everyday with the unknown and fear. Keep your thoughts in perspective. Be grateful for all everyone in your life. This day is a blessing. Let your loved ones know you care. Help others whenever, and however you can. Have a talk with God before you get too far into your day. He is waiting to hear from you. May this be a blessed day for you. May something very special come your way! Today is a gift for you. Get your party started!

July 17:
GOOD MORNING! Welcome to your day. Today may just be the best day of your life. Something special may just be presented to you; which will change your life. Do you watch for the opportunities which may come your way? Do you listen more or talk more. Are your eyes open so you can see things as they really are? Good opportunities do not come everyday. You should always be watchful and alert for them. It just takes one action to make a positive change in your life. May today be that day which brings a special opportunity to you. May you also recognize it and absorb it. This day is a gift from God. Make the most of every minute and be happy in it. Share your happiness with others. Someone may need to hear a kind word from you today to change their whole life for the better. We are here to be happy and help others. Make it happen!

July 18:
GOOD MORNING! Today you may have to deal with situations which you do not want to deal with. You may need to deal with people you do not want to deal with. Think before you speak. Do not react to something, someone may say; which you do not like. You may need to walk away and address the situation a little later. Once your words leave your mouth they cannot be put back. Some do not care how others feel or what they say to others. These are sad people. They are empty and do not feel good about themselves. It is not your job to change them. You can only change yourself. Feel good about yourself by treating others well and helping others whenever you can. This day is a gift and should not be wasted on negativity. Deal with what you have to, then move on. When you spend time on negativity from the past, you are allowing someone, or something, from the past to hurt you again. Rise above it and do not look back. This is your day. Spend it with positive people and positive actions. People love you and are waiting to hear from you. Enjoy this day as the gift it is. Get your party started!

July 19:
GOOD MORNING! Your presence has already made this day special. There are people looking forward to seeing you today; as well as hearing your voice. There are people who look up to you; whether you know it or not. Be supportive of others, rather than

critical. God has special plans for you. This plan will effect at least one other person's life in a positive way. Sometimes this plan does not come into play until much later in life. Sometimes that plan comes into life very early on. Just as we have no control over the weather we really do not control the many trials which will come our way. We will have decisions to make. This is when you need to look to God's law for answers. Man's answers and rules will change with the man. God's law never changes. This is why we have so much chaos in the world right now. Man is trying to make his own laws and they are changing to suit the man. May your decisions be wise and with the right guidance. Do not let others guide you to decisions you know are wrong. This is why we were all given the ability to make our own decisions. There are consequences for all of our decisions. Let this be a great day for you and all of those who look to you. Speak kindly to others. Help others when you can. Be an asset in the world. It is your new day. Go get it and celebrate!

July 20:

GOOD MORNING! May today be a blessed day for you and your loved ones. May you be successful in your endeavors, wise in your decisions and strong in your faith. If you were to stand before God today, how would He describe your life? Make your life count for something good. Everyday, that passes is a day closer to meeting God. Do not ignore Him. Talk with Him today. It may be your last chance. Tomorrow is not a guarantee. Make the most of this day. Today is a gift. Go get it!

July 21:

GOOD MORNING! Welcome to the newest day of your life. Today is a gift and should not be wasted on negative thoughts, angry feelings, feelings of resentment, feelings of jealousy, thoughts of vindictiveness, or feelings of chaos and turmoil. This day, and all days, should be spent on positive thoughts, feelings of happiness, feelings of generosity, and feelings of peace, joy and contentment. It really is not that hard to have these. It takes a belief and love of God and self respect. Life is too short to waste even a minute. May this be the greatest day of your life. May something very special come your way. May you also have the peace and joy you were meant to have. It is your day. Go ahead and get your party started!

July 22:
GOOD MORNING! Glad to see you have another day to share with others. Before you leave home or others leave you this morning, let them know you care. Lives change in a blink of an eye. You really have no control over what may come your way today. The two things you can control are your attitude and character. Those are both entirely dependent on yourself. If your life is filled with negativity, expect negative things to consume your life. If your character is that of someone not to be trusted then do not expect to be respected. Eliminate the negative from your life; whether it be your thoughts, actions or even people. Let those voids be filled with positive thoughts, actions and people. People that do this never have a bad day. They appreciate every day of their lives. Deceitful people are not people who are trusted or included in others lives. It only takes one dishonest action to label a person. You were meant to be happy and productive in this world. Do not allow the actions or words of others to effect you or your day. Thank God for what he has given you and may this be the greatest day of your life. Today is a gift. Go ahead and get your party started!

July 23:
GOOD MORNING! Here is a hope and prayer this is a great day for you. Do not allow others to bully you into actions you have reservations about. That is defeating the purpose of the brain God has given you. Be true to yourself. Be the person you were meant to be. If your friends want you to be someone else, then it is time to find real friends. Have plans to reach your goals and do not expect someone else to do the work for you. May you receive as you give. Treat people as you want to be treated. Tangible items can be replaced. Loved ones are not replaceable. May the memories others have of you, if you were to pass today be good. No one is perfect and we all have done things we wish we could do over. Learn from those times and excel in the good things. This day is a gift from God. Make every minute count for something good. It's your day, get your party started!

July 24:
GOOD MORNING! Looks like you have been blessed with a new day. Maybe today you can set aside some time and just thank God for this day and all the days you have been given. Maybe you could ask Him what He has in mind for your life. Maybe you could thank Him for what you have been given. Maybe you could thank Him

for the loved ones you have in your life. Maybe you could thank Him for allowing you to live in this country rather than a third world environment. You are not in this world by accident. You are here because God planned for you to be here. You have a purpose and a reason in being here. Maybe, it would be better to thank Him today. Whether, you believe in Him or not, He knows you. May this be a blessed day for you and your loved ones. May you be protected from harm and given guidance for your decisions. May this be the greatest day of your life. Today is a gift. Make the most of every minute!

July 25:
GOOD MORNING! Congratulations, it appears you have been blessed with another day. May something truly special come your way. May you and your loved ones be protected from harm and may you be given guidance for your decisions. May your eyes be open to actions around you. May you have success in your business. May your heart be filled with the joy you were meant to have. May you have the courage to speak up when you should and the wisdom to know when to keep thoughts to yourself. May you be given the opportunity to help others today. May you be generous in giving of your time and money to help others. May you be honest in your dealings and fair with others. May you receive as you give. May this be a blessed day for you. This day is truly a gift. Make it count for something good!

July 26:
GOOD MORNING! Waking up should be the biggest hurdle of the day. From here on, it should only a joy. No matter what you have going on, there is good in your life and that is what you should focus on; not the little hurdles of life. Make this a great day for yourself and everyone you come into contact with. Smile and speak to those you pass. Be humble; yet, proud of who you are. Let those you care about, know you care. You may not have another chance. You just never know what may happen in your life. Start the day with a prayer and thank God for who you are and those around you. This day is a gift. Go ahead and get your party started!

July 27:
GOOD MORNING! Your newest day has begun. Whether you have learned what purpose God has in mind for you in this world or not; everyday there needs to be a purpose, or a goal, in mind. Goals, or a purpose, gives people a reason to exist and be productive. Without a purpose, or a goal, lives would be empty and there would not be much of a reason to exist or be productive. Most have goals, or a purpose, in mind everyday. Most of those who have a purpose or a goal in mind for the day, make it a positive goal. Those are productive and generally, happy people. They have direction. When people lose sight of their goals, or purpose, they become lost and without direction. Often they fill that void with negative actions, negative behavior and unhappiness. Keep a goal, or purpose, in the forefront of your mind today. Let this be a day of happiness. When given the chance; give someone else a purpose or a goal today. Let them know you care. Give them a hug. That one little action may give the purpose they need to turn their day and even their lives for the better. May this be the greatest day of your life. God has blessed you with this day, maybe you can bless someone else's day. It's your day. Make it a good one!

July 28:
GOOD MORNING! Today may be a good day to practice patience. Be patient with all things in life. You do not know what someone else may be going through. You are only responsible for your actions, behavior and words. If your words cannot be calm, it might be best to be silent. Give thought to your words before letting loose with a barrage of insults or insinuations if you feel insulted. Once out, the words cannot be put back. You may deeply hurt someone and they may never forget or forgive you for those few moments in your life. Speak kindly to everyone. Be patient in your reactions to others and to all things in life. Live your life without regret. May this be a special day for you and may you be blessed beyond your expectations. May your eyes be open, your mind sharp and your words kind. Share your joy with others. May this be the greatest day of your life!

July 29:
GOOD MORNING! Let today be the gateway to the rest of your life. Open the doors to your success, happiness and spiritual faith in God. We are in this world to be happy. So, be happy. Do what you can about the hurdles, then turn the issues over to God,

through your faith. It is harder for some, more than others, to let go of the control of your life. There are only certain aspects of your life you really have control over. Do the best you can at whatever you do. Be honest with others. Help others whenever you can. Speak kindly to others. Let others know you care. Sometimes people forget, everyone puts their pants on one leg at a time. Don't feel like you are better than others or others are better than you. The decisions you make in your life will be with you as long as you are here. Seek guidance for the difficult ones. This is your new day to your new life. Make the most of it and go ahead and get this party started!

July 30:
GOOD MORNING! It would be so nice not to have the challenges you must face on occasion. Sometimes those challenges are the dread of the day and sometimes you may feel like you cannot deal with some of the situations which come your way. So many people have lost their spirituality and are making decisions on their desires rather than what is right or wrong. Sometimes there are not any good answers to decisions that you may have to make. Sometimes the decisions have to based on the least damaging results. The question is, "The least damaging to who, or what?" This is when the true character of a person might be revealed. People will throw friendships, or even family members, out the window for their personal desires. The irony of these types of situations is that the benefit is usually temporary anyway. The hurt, or damage, is much longer. Give thought to your decisions today. Is the result of your decision worth the pain it may cause someone else? Is it worth the damage you may do to your own character? May this be a great day for you! May your eyes and ears be open and may you be protected from harm! This day is a gift. Appreciate it and thank God for it. Go get it!

July, 31:
GOOD MORNING! This is going to be a great day for you. Get your coffee, juice, tea or whatever it is you like to start your day with; step outside and take a deep breath and just listen to sounds in the air this morning! Take a few moments to appreciate how great life is and all that is going on in the world around you. Then go on out there and be a part of that wonderful world and all it has to offer. Ignore the negative and surround yourself with positive. Someone has to be the happiest at work, at school, or just around

the neighborhood today. It just may as well be you. Feel like you have been rejected lately. Look at it as one step closer to your goal. You have to get through the no's before you get to that yes. A large portion of life is about your attitude. Make it good. God has given you this day. Make it special. Enjoy every minute. It's your day. Go ahead and get your party started!

August 1:
GOOD MORNING! Some people will have to deal with some terrible and unfortunate situations in their lives. It may be health has effected someone close to you, it may be an accident, it could be the unexpected passing of a loved one or family member. It may be financial situations like so many have experienced. These situations have a tendency of turning the path of what you may have planned for your life, or the life of someone else. Whatever the situation is, you have been given the strength to deal with it. You may have to dig deep for that strength. There may be times when you have to dig deeper than you ever have before. You will find the strength. Do not give up. God's children are never given more than they can deal with. God just has another plan in mind for you. It may not have anything to do with the plans you had. It may be you are to touch just one special person down the road. It may be you are to touch many. Rest assured, everything happens for a reason. It may not be what you had you planned; then again, you can only control your attitude, not what comes at you in life. Stay strong in those tough times. In the end, you will look back and realize that situation was not as bad as it seemed. May this be the greatest day of your life. May you be blessed with good health, wisdom and guidance. Let those you love, know you care. Make the most of every minute. Go ahead and get your day started!

August 2:
GOOD MORNING! Here's a hope and a prayer; today is a safe day for you. May it be productive and may you and your loved ones return home as you left. Let your loved ones know you care and enjoy this day as the gift it is. It is all up to you. Go get it!

August 3:
GOOD MORNING! Welcome to the newest day of your life. May this be the greatest day for you and your loved ones. Think only positive, say only positive and be only positive. Do your best at everything you do; whether, you want to do it or not. Everything, at every moment, should be approached as the most important accomplishment you will ever have. Sometime today, take the time to thank God for your day and your loved ones. It is your day. Make it the best you can!

August 4:
GOOD MORNING! It's a new day. This is a great day to open the doors of happiness you are to have in this life. Let go of any anger and resentment you may be carrying, or harboring. Those emotions use up time and space in your life and are non productive. Open your heart to helping others, do the best you can at whatever you do, be positive in your words and humble in your behavior, and have an appreciation for the life you have. Make every minute count today. This day is a gift. Enjoy it as it was given!

August 5:
GOOD MORNING! Looks like you have been given another day. This also means you are one day closer to your final day here. It also means those you care about are one day closer to their finals days. You may never know when your final day will come. When young, most feel they will live forever. As life goes on people start to realize just how short life is and there is an end to it. If you knew today was your final day in this world just how would you spend your last moments? Would you call those who mean the most to you and tell them "goodbye?" Would you spend your time with those you care the most about? Would you waste that time or make what just might be the most important time in your life, the best time of your life? Why wait until that day comes? Live everyday like it is your last. Be kind to everyone you meet and be happy within yourself. Those who have faith in God will be looking forward to their end time. Those who do not have faith will be concerned about the unknown and the darkness they may be expecting to come. How will your last day be? May this be a great day for you and may you be blessed with good health, wisdom, patience and contentment. Live this day to it's fullest!

August 6:
GOOD MORNING! Spend your time on the important things in life. Thank God for being here and giving you the loved ones you have. Spend your time on things that matter. Spend your time on positive things. Let go of the things and people who would hinder you. You are never to old to learn. Feel good about who you are. You are loved and you are here for a special reason. Fight the important battles. May you be blessed beyond your wishes. May your health be good, your eyes open, and your mind clear. This day is a gift. Go ahead and get your party started!

August 7:
GOOD MORNING! Like others, you may have some moments from the past which you would like to go back and change. Everyone has experienced some point in their life when they wish they could go back and relive certain times and make different decisions. Needless, to say, you do not have that ability. There are consequences for all of actions. Good actions, usually mean good consequences. Bad decisions, usually mean someone is going to suffer; whether, it be you or someone else. These are the times you learn from. These are the times which help make you the person you are. Do not let anger, or hurt from those times continue to affect your life. Today is the first day of the rest of your life. Put the past to rest and move on. The sun is coming up and today is a gift. Enjoy it and make the best of every minute you have!

August 8:
GOOD MORNING! Here's hoping you slept well and feel great peace today. If you are carrying anger everyday, you will never know true peace and happiness. Everyone has been hurt at one time or another in their lives. You may have experienced some terrible things in your life. There may be one situation which has burdened you more than any other. Until you forgive the person who committed that hurt, it will always be a hurt to you. You do not have to forget. You do not have to be someone's best buddy. You do need to forgive and move on. Every time the anger rises you are being hurt again. Do not let an action or a person continue to hurt you. Do not allow another to have power over you. Let it go. Christians believe Jesus Christ died on the cross so our sins would be forgiven. If he could do that for millions of people he did not know, is forgiving another possible for you? May this be the day you let go of all the anger you may be carrying. Fill that part of your life with positive and feel the difference. May this be the greatest day of your life!

August 9:
GOOD MORNING! Here's hoping you slept well and are ready this new day. Do everything to your best. Listen more than you speak. Help others whenever you have the opportunity. Smile and speak to those you pass. Let this be a happy day for you. Let others know you care. No matter what is coming today; tomorrow is another day! Thank God for the gift of this day!

August 10:
GOOD MORNING! May this be a great day for you. May you have the confidence in yourself to laugh at those who would hurt you. May you have the compassion to help those in need. May you have the wisdom to know what is really important in life. May you have the appreciation for your life and know what a true miracle you are. If you have not found that, "special purpose" in your life; may today be the day you find it. Life is short; make the most of every moment and let those you love, know it. May this be the greatest day of your life. May you be blessed with all that is good!

August 11:
GOOD MORNING! Looks like you have been given a new day. May you get as you give today. Know a person by their actions, not their words. All days are good; some are just better than others. Help those in need. Start and end your day with a prayer of thanks. Enjoy your new day as the gift it is. Go ahead and get your party started!

August 12:
GOOD MORNING! So good to have you here today. Although, you can control your reactions to situations; you have no control over many of the things that will happen in your life. The same holds true for your daily attitude. Many are suffering today in situations which they had no control over. For some, this may have been going on for years. It will wear on the best of people, if they allow it. Sooner or later, you will come to a point in your life when you will need divine intervention to get you through a situation; or a strength from more than you can physically get from this world. These are situations which are not planned on, but everyone has them. Who are you going to look to for guidance, strength or help? Your day is coming. I hope and pray you are ready and know where to go. Those who know God suffer the least. May this be a most blessed day for you and your loved ones. Share your happiness and joy with others. Help those you can. Let those you love know it. Make the most of every minute of this day! Get your party started!

August 13:

GOOD MORNING! You may be one the many people who need some extra support today. You may be having the toughest time in your life. You may be having to make decisions you never thought you would have to make. No matter what you are having to deal with, there are people who have been where you are now. There are also people who have it worse than you. There are people who care about you and will help, if you let them. There is also good guidance for you if you seek it from the right places. May your eyes be open, your mind clear and your health good. Do not let anger control your actions. Make this a good day for you, at least in attitude! You are here and that is a great start. Glad to see you! You are important!

August 14:

GOOD MORNING! Welcome to the first day of the rest of your life. Today would be a great day to begin the journey of happiness of the rest of your life; if you have not already. Appreciate everything you have, no matter how small or how few. Appreciate your loved ones and the true friends you have. Appreciate the ability to breathe, walk, talk, smell, taste, sight and touch. Do not take these things for granted. If you are blessed to have any or all of the above you are already blessed. Start your day with a prayer and do something different and for yourself this am. Take a walk, step outside and listen to all the life going on around you, or just sit quietly and have a talk with God or your guardian angels. Smile and speak to everyone you pass. Get to know those you have contact with, throughout the day. There are some wonderful and beautiful people out there. Share your happiness and beauty with others, Do not keep it to yourself. Know you are loved and you are special. Make today the beginning of the happiest part of your life! Today is a gift, go ahead and get your party started!

August 15:

GOOD MORNING! Welcome and congratulations on the newest day of your life. You probably remember people who influenced you from many, many years ago in your life. It may have been a relative, a teacher or a friend. Chances are high, that influence had a positive effect on you and your life. You may also have influenced others in your life; just as someone influenced you. You may be admired just as you admire someone else. It could be something small you did or said to someone. It could also be your lifestyle or the way you conduct your life; which, effected someone else's life. You will leave a path as you go through life. Is your path going to be thoughts of good memories or chaos and disasters? You cannot control what situations may come into your life. You can control how you deal with the situations. Live without regret. May this be the greatest day of your life. Show others you care and smile a lot. You are blessed. Make the best of your life. It is short!

August 16:
GOOD MORNING! So good to see you have another day in this world. May it be a great day for you. May you and your loved ones be safe. May you be blessed with wisdom, patience and compassion towards others. May your heart and mind be open to new things. May your health be good and may you receive as you give. Be positive and carry no negative feelings. Know you are loved and you have a special reason to be in this world. Today is a gift; enjoy it as it was given.

August 17:
GOOD MORNING! Welcome to the newest day of your life! May this day be a blessed day for you. May something truly special and unexpected come your way. May you be able to give something today that no one could ever pay your for. May you meet someone today who always be special in your life. May you know true happiness and contentment! May this be the greatest day of your life! Enjoy and make the best of every minute!

August 18:
GOOD MORNING! There are some days when things just may seem to be working against you. No matter what you do, or how you do it, there seems to be a roadblock or a new hurdle in the road. These are the days when patience may be the most valuable of your traits. Patience may be what keeps you moving forward in your life. Patience may keep you on your path to success. Patience may also keep you from lashing out at a loved one or someone not responsible for the hurdles you are facing. Patience may keep you smiling. Your patience can be a key to your success and a good attitude. Try to keep in mind, what ever you are experiencing, someone has already been there. Releasing the stress from the tough times; can be done through prayer. Patience will help your attitude remain good. May you be protected from harm. May you be blessed. May you be content and may your heart be full of the joy

it was meant to have. This day is a gift. It is up to you to enjoy the party!

August 19:
GOOD MORNING! It is so good to see you have another day. Live this day like it is your last. Make the most of every minute. Treat your loved ones like this is the last day you will be able to see them. Smile like tomorrow is the start of a vacation. Start and end the day with a prayer. This day is a gift. Get your party started!

August 20:
GOOD MORNING! Looks like you have a new day to enjoy. Since you are here the day has already started off well. You can just make this another great day. Most people have a different way of seeing things. Seeing things differently does not make one right or one wrong. The same goes for opinions. Everyone has a different opinion about different things. Keep this in mind when it comes to being around others. Enjoy this day and enjoy your time with others; especially, the loved ones. Do your best at everything you do. Make this day count for something!

August 21:
GOOD MORNING! Welcome to the newest day of your life. Keep things in perspective today. Make sure what gets you excited, is worth getting excited about. Speak kindly to others. Show others you care. You are needed in this world and you are loved. Start the day with a prayer and carry no negative baggage. This day is a gift. Go ahead and get your party started!

August 22:
GOOD MORNING! There will be some who will pass from this world today. Families and loved ones will be left in pain and with a void in their lives. In these times; it is important to consider the good times which were shared and the blessings in having these people in your life. The pain never stops. The loss will become easier to deal with as time goes on. It will be important to begin focussing on the other blessings in your life. Life is short. Appreciate what you have and who you have in your life while you have them. Tomorrow may be completely different from today. Make every minute count. Start your day with a prayer. You just may feel better. Enjoy this day as the gift it is. May this be the best day of your life.

August 23:
GOOD MORNING! Oh good! A new day! It is so good to be alive. Stretch, breathe deep and listen to the sounds outside. If you have a furry friend, they are probably dancing around your feet, wiggling back and forth, maybe jumping up to be petted, or just touched. They love you unconditionally, and live to be with, and please, you. People should be so dedicated to their loved ones. You should be happy to see them, morning, day, or night. You can learn a lot from your's, or other's, furry friends. Let others know you care. A warm handshake when you run into someone you know. A hug to someone might just make their day. Take the time to get to know others. Everyone is different and comes from different backgrounds. May this be the greatest day of your life. May the hands of God protect you while your faith gives you strength. Keep your attitude positive and leave no room for negative feelings. Thank God for the day and get your party started!

August 24:
GOOD MORNING! Welcome to the newest day of your life. So glad to see you here today. Keep your heart and mind open to positive and good things. The more positive around you the more positive you will be. A positive person can take on anything. Do not let others drag you into their misery or drama. God gave you a brain for a reason. Use it. If you feel like you are running into a wall, go around it. Do not wait for others. Move forward and move on. May this be the most blessed day on your life. Today, is a gift. Now, you can get your party started!

August 25:
GOOD MORNING! Looks like you have been blessed with a new day. If you see a person in need, would you help that person or avoid them? Do you speak to someone who might appear to be homeless or avoid them? Never look down on another. There are many out there who are in situations beyond their control. Everyone is a brother, sister, father, mother, daughter or son to another. Help others when you have the opportunity. Do not wait to be asked. Do not ever feel, "That, could never be me." Your life can change in the blink of an eye. May you be blessed beyond your dreams today. This day is a gift. Make the most of every minute and help those you can. You just never know when you may need help.

August 26:
GOOD MORNING! May this be the greatest day of your life. May you be at peace with all that comes your way, good and bad. May you be an inspiration to others and may you have the opportunity to do something good to help another today. May you be blessed with good health, guidance and wisdom for your decisions. Today is a gift. Make the best of every minute and enjoy this day!

August 27:
GOOD MORNING! So glad to see you. You have entered another day. Today you can make all things good. No matter what comes your way; you have the ability to overcome and surpass all things. You just need the desire. If you are without negativity in your life, then you are filled with positive. Nothing can hold you back. Start and end your day with prayer and thankfulness. Learn from the mistakes and keep moving forward. This day is a gift. Share a smile with someone who needs it. Just a few minutes of your time may mean more than you know to another. Let others know you care. May this be the greatest day of your life. There are others who love you and need you. Wait for no one. This is your day. Get your party started!

August 28:
GOOD MORNING! Here's a hope and prayer this is a great day for you. May your conflicts be few. May your guidance and wisdom be good. May your day be filled with positive thoughts and actions. You were made special for a special reason. Be proud of who you are and do not change who you are to please someone else. May this be a great day for you and your loved ones. Get on out there and make this day as it was meant to be. A gift and a blessing!

August 29:
GOOD MORNING! Congratulations on the first day, of the rest of your life! Be slow to anger in all matters. Anger does not solve any problems, may make things worse and has been the end of many relationships. Think before you speak. You are meant to have peace, happiness and contentment in your heart and life. You can-not have any of these if you are carrying anger around with you. Let it go and move on through your life. Do not let something or others have control over you. Do everything to the best of your ability and you will be at peace with yourself. May you find your

purpose in life and may you have the opportunity to help another today. Start and end the day with a prayer. Know you are loved.

August 30:
GOOD MORNING! Welcome to the newest day of your life. You have already made this day special; just by being here. Take the time to appreciate what you have been given. Look at your loved ones, your health, and your heart. You cannot put a price on any of these. They are your most valuable possessions. Your loved ones and your health are obvious. What is in your heart is not always so obvious. You are meant to be happy in this world. Only you can truly know how you feel with your heart. You should feel good about waking up and enjoying the gift of life. If happiness is not in your life; then, perhaps, something about your life needs to change. Start your day with a prayer. Thank God for what you have. Then dance and sing your way through your day. You are here for a purpose. Once that purpose has been fulfilled your job in this world will be complete. Live every minute like it is your last. May you be blessed with good health and true happiness today. Enjoy this gift and go ahead and get your party started!

August 31:
GOOD MORNING! It's a new day to start your life over. Get your coffee, tea, or morning go juice, stretch and take in a deep breath of oxygen and step outside and listen to miracles of life. Be silent for just a minute and have an appreciation for being here. Thank God for this gift. Now you are ready. Go get it. It is yours and this day is starting to roll along. Forget about the negatives from yesterday and make today better. Help those you can and speak to all you meet. This day is a gift. It is up to you what you make of it! Get your party started!

September 1:
GOOD MORNING! Congratulations on your newest day! Everyday
you have, will be one day closer to the end of your time in this
world. Many never know when that time will come. It is tragic
when someone, unexpectedly, is taken from this world. Every action you are involved with could be the last impression you will
leave in this world such as: a picture someone takes at a family get
together, an afternoon drive with someone special, helping someone who is need, a conversation with a close friend. When your job
is finished in this world, your time here will come to an end. If you
keep this in mind as you go through your life, you will be loved and
respected while you are here and well remembered in the end. Fill
your life with positive thoughts, words and actions. You will be
happy and those around you will be happier because of you. May
this be the greatest day of your life. May you be blessed beyond
your desires. Being positive is up to you. This is your day. Go get
it!

September 2:
GOOD MORNING! So, your day is here and begins. A positive day
should begin and end with positive reinforcement. Starting the day
with a prayer and thanking God for all you have will always be a
good start. Keep in mind the most valuable things are those you
cannot pay for. Your health, your loved ones, your eyesight, hearing, being able to feel and walk are all things which make life so
much better. Keep in mind how blessed you are as you go through
the day. This will make situations and people so much better to
deal with. You can turn bad situations into "not so bad" situations.
You may even calm others when they realize you have control over
your emotions. Also, let those who are special to you, know you
care. At the end of the day, thank God for being with and protect-
ing you throughout the day. This will give you a good day! May you
touch someone's heart today and lift their spirits. May you receive
as you give. This is your day. Take good care of it!

September 3:
GOOD MORNING! So glad to see you today. It appears you have
been given a new day with possibly new challenges and new situations, some good and some not so good. The outcome of these situations will sometimes be good and sometimes not so good. No
one is perfect and everyone makes mistakes. It important to acknowledge and accept your mistakes and then learn from them.

Waking up was God's first gift to you today. Keep your attitude good and have an appreciation for all the gifts that come your way. May this be the greatest day of your life. May something truly special come your way. Know you are loved and needed in this world. Go ahead and get your day started. The world will be a lot better with you in it today. Thank you for being here!

September 4:
GOOD MORNING! Good morning and welcome to the newest day of your life. If there is something you've wanted to do and have procrastinated starting; today is a great day to start. Every great plan has a starting point. Let today be the starting point of something you have been putting off. Procrastination is another form of "I do not deserve" or "I am not worthy." You deserve everything you work for. Do your best at everything you do and you will feel much better about your accomplishments and yourself. You are here to be successful and productive. You may not be successful at all the attempts but you do learn. May you succeed with a special accomplishment today. May that accomplishment be good for you and/or others. Life is short. Make the best of every minute. The next minute is not a guarantee.

September 5:
GOOD MORNING! Let this be a day of contentment and peace for you. Smile and tackle the challenges that you face today. Do not give up. Sometimes, you have to look for another way around the issues. There is a power working against you all the time. Be stronger than that power. Call on God to help you through those times. Whether you know Him or not; He knows you. God answers the prayers of those who believe in Him. May this be a blessed day for you and your loved ones. May this be the greatest day of your life!

September 6:
GOOD MORNING! Welcome and so glad to see you today. The good news of the day is, you are only responsible for yourself and can only change yourself. That means you do not have to be concerned with the behavior of others and you can focus on improving yourself today. If you are already feeling perfect, you may not feel the love from others like you should anyway. It is a great time to begin sharing your appreciation with others with a smile and

speaking to those you pass. You never know just how much a "hel-lo" may mean to someone else. Thank you for being here!

September 7:
GOOD MORNING! Today, you will need to overlook the disap-pointments which come with life. Your reactions to those disap-pointments is what helps to define you. If you dwell on the nega-tive; there will have a negative impact in your life. You do your best and accept the consequences. Live to fight another day. Win-ning all the battles is not what is important. Today is a new day and there are people wanting to see you and hear your voice. The world is a better place with you in it. Make the most of the next minute. Once it passes, it will be gone. May this be a blessed day for you and your loved ones. May you be protected from harm and may your decisions be wise. Today is a gift. It is time to your party started!

September 8:
GOOD MORNING! Welcome to the newest day of your life. You have been given this day because you have a purpose in this world. You are needed to help someone, or many, while here. Your pres-ence makes it a better day for others. If you have not found the "special purpose" for your life, today may be the day. Start your day with a prayer and thank God for those you are close to. Take a few minutes and talk to someone you have missed. They are prob-ably missing you too. May this be a great day for you and your loved ones. So glad you are here today!

September 9:
GOOD MORNING! It is good you are here today. Sometimes, it may feel like the whole world is coming in on you. It may be health issues. It may be financial. It could be family or more personal is-sues. You will have those times; just as you will have the times when you feel on top of the world. No matter what, the sun will come up tomorrow and tomorrow will be a new day. Do not judge your life by one day or even a month. Life is good. It is your atti-tude which makes it a good day or a bad day. May this be the a good day for you. May your attitude be so good you have enough good to lift someone else up. May you be a positive inspiration to others! Enjoy this day. It is a gift!

September 10:
GOOD MORNING! Looks as though your job is still not done here and God has given you another day. We are here to be happy. We are here to be productive and to help each other. We are here to worship God. His hand of protection is slowly being lifted as a few are allowed to remove his name from our society. Do not allow others to tell you how you should feel. Keep your heart right. A day of reckoning is coming. He is not expecting perfection. He is wanting your belief and faith. That is all he is asking for. He knows you already. You will call on him one day. Do not wait until it is too late. May this be a blessed day for you and your loved ones....

September 11:
GOOD MORNING! A new day has arrived. This is a wonderful gift to be given. Use it to do positive things with positive thoughts. May this be a great day for you. May you be blessed with good health, wisdom, and time with your loved ones. This is your day. Make the most of every minute. Go ahead and get your party started!

September 12:
GOOD MORNING! You have already started the day off well. You are alive. You may have issues in your life which are trying to drag you down. You may feel like you are facing the worst day of your life. No matter what, someone has been where you are right now. The sun came up for them, the next day, as it will for you. We have bad things happen to us throughout our lives. Some are self induced, some are completely outside our control. You will get through it. You do your best and move on. Having a little word of prayer helps. If you are having a situation in your life which is causing more hurt and frustration than you have experienced; keep in mind, no matter what it is, it is temporary. May you and your loved ones be blessed beyond your hopes today. Today is a gift. Enjoy and make the best of every minute!

September 13:
GOOD MORNING! It's a new day and so glad to see you here today. If you are able to get out and about, think about those who may not be so lucky. Share a little of your time today with someone who may not be as mobile as you. Make a phone call. Stop by and visit. One day you may be wishing someone would spend a little time with you. Enjoy this day. Share your joy with others. Smile

and speak to those you pass. This day is a gift. Appreciate it and treat it well! It's your gift. Go get it!

September 14:
GOOD MORNING! You have been blessed with a special talent or trait. That talent or trait, is for that special purpose you have in this life. Once you realize what your "special purpose" in this life is, you will be secure in being who you are. Part of that security is being able to accept and acknowledge you are not perfect, you make mistakes and that is ok. You do not have to blame others for something that does not go as expected. This is true self confidence. The more self confidence you have, the more positive you and your life will become. May this be a blessed day for you and your loved ones. May you find your "special purpose," if you have not. Today is a gift. Thank God for it. Do not waste any of it.

September 15:
GOOD MORNING! Good to see you here today. Hopefully, you feel as good about being in the world today as others feel good about having you here. Know you are loved and you are needed. Treat yourself to something special today. Do something with a loved one. Visit a family member or someone who is special to you. Call someone you respect and love; who you might not have connected with in a while. Face your challenges calmly and with thought. Today is a gift from God. Let him know you are thankful for the time in this world and you are thankful for your loved ones. Today is the first day of the rest of your life. Make it positive and make it count! Go ahead and get your party started!

September 16:
GOOD MORNING! Glad you are able to a part of this new day. It is always best to start the day with a prayer. Let God know you appreciate what you have and ask him for guidance for your decisions. Let your loved ones know you care before they, or you, leave the home. If possible, spend some time with those you love. Realize what is truly important in your life. Expect respect, only if you treat others with respect. May this be a blessed day for you and your loved ones. Avoid the negative. This day is a gift. Appreciate it as it was given.

September 17:
GOOD MORNING! Well, how about if you just get this day moving along. You are already blessed to be here, so take advantage of it and make it a great day. Spend some time with those who are important to you. Be your best at everything you do. Smile and speak to those you pass. Spend your time on the positive thoughts and actions. Let this be the greatest day of your life. Leave good thoughts in your path. Today is a gift. Treat it like it is appreciated. Now, go ahead and get your party started!

September 18:
GOOD MORNING! Welcome to your newest day in the miracle of life. One of the strongest of emotions is "fear." Fear comes from the dealing with the unknown. Some deal with the unknown better than others. If you allow fear to hold you back you will never know your full potential or see what you could accomplish. If you see a better way to accomplish a challenge then try it. Is there something different you want to do on your next day off; then go do it. Do not be afraid of speaking up or thinking for yourself. No one is right all the time. You are hear to enjoy life and be successful. Do not let the fear of the unknown hold you back. Make this a positively memorable day for yourself or someone else. Do something good for someone else today. May you receive as you give. Enjoy this miracle of a day and be blessed!

September 19:
GOOD MORNING! Looks like you have been blessed with another day in this world. Enjoying the day is more about attitude than anything else. It does not matter what may come into your life; your attitude can make it a good day or a bad day. You cannot have a good attitude if you are carrying anger. You have to learn to be forgiving. Let go of any anger towards others and move on. Carrying anger just allows someone to hurt you over and over again. May something truly special and unexpected come your way today. May you and your loved ones be blessed beyond your dreams. May your heart be opened to others and may you have the opportunity to help another. Smile and speak to others. You have a purpose in this world and you are loved. Today is a gift. Go ahead and make the best of this day. You are only going to get this chance once!

September 20:
GOOD MORNING! So glad to see you have another day in this world. There are two ways to go through this day. You can enjoy and embrace being here and all that comes with it; or, you can dwell on the negative and drag yourself through the day. This choice is yours. May you be blessed beyond your hopes and prayers. May your positive outlook provide you with new doors to open. Thank God for what you have and start and end the day with a prayer. This is your day. Go get it and get your party started!

September 21:
GOOD MORNING! Looks like you have been given a new day to enjoy. Many people will leave home today and not return. Many will leave their home and return in a much different condition. These situations happen because of health, accidents, and even intentional causes. Once a life changing situation arises, it may be too late to really appreciate what you have and what you can do with what you have been given. Be glad for what God has given you. Enjoy everyday to the best of your ability. You are in this world for a reason. Get on out there and explore what life has to offer. Make the most of your days. Be your best at everything you do. Make this day count for something special. Today is a gift. Enjoy it and may this be the greatest day of your life!

September 22:
GOOD MORNING: It is so good to see you will have a new day in this world. It is important to complete everything you do to the best of your ability. Whether you are doing something for yourself, at home, or at work; you should always put 100% of your effort behind the "task." By completing everything you do well; you are showing others you feel good about yourself and what you can do. You will also feel better about yourself and what you can accomplish. Start your day with a prayer and thank God for being here and the life you have. May you find the confidence and happiness that are yours to have. May this be the greatest day of your life. Your clock is ticking. Make every minute count!

September 23:
GOOD MORNING! It is good you are here today. You may know of someone who has had an accident, health issues or is elderly, and is not as mobile as they once were. Many people have been put into "homes" where they can get 24 hour care. Some may be

blessed with a caretaker in their own homes. It was not that long ago, people stayed with family until they left this world. Today is a good day to let people know they are not forgotten and are loved. If you know of someone who may be elderly, sick or immobile, let them know they are loved and you care. You may be in that position one day. Just pick up the phone or stop by. The few minutes you take from your day may give more happiness to someone than you could possibly know. Make the best of this day. It is a blessing. May you get as you give. May something truly special come your way today.

September 24:
GOOD MORNING! It's time to get that body moving and join the world. Looks like you have been blessed with another day. It is not just another day; it is a new day. Learn from the mistakes of yesterday and let go of anything negative. That negative stuff is like an anchor holding you down or back. Set your goal and make it happen. Not everything is going to happen the way you want it too. Not everything is going to be as easy as you want it to be. These are what you call lessons of life. These help make you the person you are. When things don't go the way you want, just say, "thank you God" and move on. Do not forget to thank Him when things do go your way. Let those you love, know you care. Let those you meet, know you care also. Sometimes just a smile will make someone's worst day better. May you enjoy every minute of this day to it's fullest! This is your day, go get it!

September 25:
GOOD MORNING! Life is great. It is the living of life which can be rough. It is a lot easier if you keep yourself from being pulled into others' drama and do not allow yourself to, instantly, react to stressful situations. Always consider your words and actions before speaking. Once the words come out they cannot be put back. Make this a special day for yourself or someone else. Think about the good things and smile as you go through the day. Remember there are others who would rather be in your shoes than facing what they are. May this be the greatest day of your life. May you be blessed beyond your hopes, desires and prayers. Today is a gift and it is time to get the party started!

September 26:
GOOD MORNING! It appears you have been given another, new, day to be happy and to spread your happiness to others. If you look around, it will not take long to see someone who is in some distress over some chaos or situation in their life. Take the time to let others know you care. A smile or just a few sincere and positive words from you may change the entire day of someone who is in pain. There is no need to give advice; unless, asked. Nothing shows you care more than a hug. Everyone measures pain at different levels. What may be devastating to one may not be as hurtful to another. It is more important to just let others know you care and you are there for them. Christians will offer a word of prayer. Ultimately, most will turn to God for help at some point. May this be a truly great day for you. May you and your loved ones return home as good or better than you left. Make the best of every minute. Go ahead and get your party started!

September 27:
GOOD MORNING! Welcome to the newest day of your life. You are meant to be happy in this world. You will have some ups and downs. Today, just decide to look at the ups and make the most of every minute. Be positive and do not rush to judgements. Enjoy this day and all it has to offer. May this be the greatest day of your life. Start your day with a prayer and appreciate what you have been given. Now, go ahead and get your party started!

September 28:
GOOD MORNING! Waking up has already made this a great day. Appreciate this day and be glad in all you have. Start your day with a prayer. Sooner or later, you will need more strength than you have ever needed. You may want to consider who and where you will be looking for that strength. Most will turn to God. You may want to reach out to him before that day comes. He just wants you to believe in him. He already knows you. Take a moment and thank him for who you are, what you have and where you have been. May this be a blessed day for you and your loved ones. May you be truly happy with yourself and all that is around you. This day is a gift. Make the most of it and get your party started!

September 29:
GOOD MORNING! So good to see you today. Make today a special day for yourself or your loved ones. Do something out of the ordinary. Go outside and listen to all the life around you. Take your shoes off and walk around. Just take a break from the routine and do something different. May this be a great day for you. May you have an appreciation for all that is living. May you be happy, content in who you are, and generous with your time to others. Go ahead and get this day started. It is a gift and it is moving on. May this be the greatest day of your life!

September 30:
GOOD MORNING! Dear Lord, I humbly come before you to thank you for this day you have given us. I ask that you continue to watch over everyone today. Guide us and show us the direction you would have us go. Protect us from harm. Travel with us today and bring us home safely. Give us the wisdom we need to make the decisions we need to make. May everyone have a chance to open their hearts and minds to you; before they leave this world. Keep temptation from us and when we must face it give us the strength to overcome it. Bless our children, parents, loved ones and friends. Forgive us of our sins and forgive this nation for turning it's back on you. May we forgive others as you forgave us. May you also lay your hands on those who may need your strength to overcome situations in their life today. We continue to pray for your protection Dear Lord and thank you for all that we have. In Jesus name I pray and ask for these things, Amen.........

October 1:
GOOD MORNING! It is time to get this day started and make good things happen. If you are waiting for good things to come to you, then you may be waiting a long time and that is wasting valuable time. You should be setting your goals and make the plans to accomplish those goals. Start and end your day with a prayer. May this be a good day for you and your loved ones. May you be safe and protected from harm. Move past those who would hurt you, or others. You will only get this day once and there are no do overs. It is also your day. Make it the best you can. May this be the best day of your life. Now go get it!

October 2:
GOOD MORNING! Welcome to your newest day on the road trip of life. Today, is a good day to acknowledge you are unable to change anyone else's behavior. You only have control over your own attitude and behavior. Focus on what you can do to improve yourself. Spend your time on what you can do with yourself and life will be much better and you will be happier. Make the most of every minute of this day. Ultimately, you do not know if you will be here tomorrow. Let your words be kind to others. Speak to those you pass. Get to know others. Know you are loved and you are in this world for a reason. Make your time count for good things. This day is a gift. Make it all you can!

October 3:
GOOD MORNING! It is so good to see you have been given a new day. If you could just give one person a day something to be happy and smile about; you've had a good day. You cannot make others happy. You can give them something which will help them feel good about themselves. A smile, a little conversation, and/or a hug will let others know you care. Start and end your day with a prayer. Appreciate what God has allowed you to have. Everyday is a blessing and they deserve your best. Never pass up an opportunity to help someone else. May this be the greatest day of your life. May you and your loved ones be protected from harm and may you return home safely. This is your day. Make it a good one!

October 4:
GOOD MORNING! Congratulations on the newest day God has given you. You are one day closer to the time you will leave this world. Some will be allowed to live long lives. Some will have only

to be here for short periods of time. Will you be remembered as a person who helped others or a person who hurt others when your time comes? Appreciate this time and day. Do everything with a smile and gratitude. Accept every opportunity to help others. Let your loved ones know you love them before you leave them. You never know what may be coming down the highway of life. May this day be the greatest day of your life. May all your wishes and prayers come true. May you be filled with the joy you were meant to have. This is your day. Go get it!

October 5:
GOOD MORNING! Your presence has already made this a special day. Whether you know it or not; there are people who look forward to you being here today. You are important to others. You are also loved by others. You do have a special purpose in this world and you also hold a special place in this world. If you have not found that special purpose yet; maybe, today will be the day. Enjoy this day and be happy in it. Ignore the drama of others and those who would hold you back. May today be a very special day for you and may your prayers be answered. Today is a gift. Appreciate how great that gift is!

October 6:
GOOD MORNING! Welcome to the newest day of your life. Glad you have been given another day in this world. You may be facing some challenging times right now. You have been given the strength to deal with those challenging times. It may seem like the end of the world; however, someone has been down that same road before you. Challenges, bring about change. Positive changes are a good thing. For every negative action there is a positive action. Sometimes, you may have to look deep and sometimes it may take time before the positive surfaces. It will be there. Late for work because you could not find your keys or a flat tire maybe? Maybe, you were being kept out of the way of a truck missing a red light. Do not allow challenges to control your life. You have been given the strength to overcome them. Keep the attitude positive. Make lemonade from the lemons in your life. This day is a gift. Please do not waste any of it. Do good things for others as well yourself. Go ahead and get your party started. This day is moving on!

October 7:
GOOD MORNING! Good to see you today. It is good you are here. Welcome this day with open arms and a smile on your face. No matter what comes at you today, know you can deal with it. Speak to those you pass. Get to know the people who cross paths with you. Help others when you have the opportunity. Start and end your day with a prayer. Say a prayer for those you know who are in need. May this be a blessed day for you. May all your words be kind and positive. May you continue to be a blessing to others. This day is a gift. Appreciate it!

October 8:
GOOD MORNING! Look who has a new day to share with others. Congratulations! Take advantage of this time and do something special with the time. Every minute that goes by is another minute less in your future. Make every one count for something good. You are here to be happy and to help others. You can make it happen. It is not that hard. Stay strong in your faith to God and anything can be done. Pray often. Let go of the negative and fill those voids with positive. You will be amazed at the change and quality of your life. This is your day and this day is the gift of the day. Go ahead and get your day started!

October 9:
GOOD MORNING! So good of you to be here today. Every minute that passes, is a minute less in your future. You will want to make the most of every minute to make the most of your life. Your time in this world, will come to an end, when your purpose in this world is complete. Often times, people do not know when that has happened. Everyone has a special purpose which may be accomplished without even being aware of it. Smile and speak to everyone you meet or pass. Be kind in your words. Be considerate of others. Carry no bad feelings or vindictiveness. Time to make things happen. This day is a blessing. Cherish every minute you have. Life is short! Go ahead and get this party started!

October 10:
GOOD MORNING! You have the ability to make this a happy day for yourself and those around you. Keep moving forward, ignore the negative around you and keep your faith. Start the day with a prayer and end it the same way. Stay close to your loved ones and let others know you care. Choose your words carefully and do not

respond in anger. Have an appreciation for life and all it brings. This day is a gift. Be grateful and share your joy with others!

October 11:
GOOD MORNING! Looks like you have another day to enjoy in this world. So glad you are here and able to do things which may not have gotten done yesterday. Do not be afraid to admit your mistakes. Everyone makes mistakes. Admitting you made one does not make a person any less a person. It does show you are secure in yourself. May this be a great day for you. May you be blessed beyond your prayers and wishes. May you return home as healthy or better than you left. Let your loved ones know you care. This is your day. Go get it!

October 12:
GOOD MORNING! A new day is here. Start the day with a prayer and a smile. Sing (if you can) do the happy dance and get the day started. Talk to someone who may not be doing as well as you today. Lift their spirits. Share some happiness with others. This day is a gift. Appreciate it and make the most of every minute.

October 13:
GOOD MORNING! Isn't it great when you first wake up and realize you are alive? It is great to see you. There are people who depend on you being here today. There are people who love you and would be heartbroken without you too. Reach out and connect with those who are important in your life. Even if it just briefly. Let others know you care. Tomorrow may be too late. Speak to and be kind to others. You never know when the last words you speak to someone may really be the last words you speak to someone. Start and end your day with a prayer. It will make the in between, better. May this be a blessed day for you and your loved ones. Get your day started. There is so much to do!

October 14:
GOOD MORNING! Everyday is a good day. Some may be a bit rougher than others. No matter what you may face or what may come your way today, tomorrow is on the horizon. You will get through this day and any issues which may come with it. The rough days are a lot easier if you have someone to talk to or someone you can release your troubles to. Christians look to God and can deal with the difficult times. Sooner or later most will call on

God for strength, help or hope. It is a humbling experience when you first feel the peace He can give you. He already knows you. If you are having a difficult time you may want to speak to God about it; even if you have never prayed before. Do not wait until it is too late. You just never know what may come at you these days. May this be a blessed day for you and your family. May you be protected from harm and may your day end as good as, or better then, it started. Today is a gift. Appreciate it, as it was given.

October 15:
GOOD MORNING! Welcome to the newest day of your life. It appears God has more planned for you and your life. You may not always have a choice in what comes your way; however, you do have a choice of how you deal with, and look at, situations you may be involved with. Carrying anger is non productive, negative and will take away from your personality. Vindictiveness is all negative and uses up space which could be used for positive things. The more positive you have in your life the less space for the negative you will have. The more positive you have; the less the negative will bother you also. There are many who have situations they cannot change. You may still be able to change your attitude, and life, if you want or need to. The decisions to lead a positive life or a negative life is up to you. It does not matter what has happened in the past. Today is the first day of the rest of your life. Start and end you day with a prayer. Now, go ahead and get your party started!

October 16:
GOOD MORNING! Ahh, a new day is here for you. Thank you Lord. Today you can finish everything you did not finish yesterday. Today, you can speak to all those you have missed speaking with, for so long. Today you can finish reading that book you started. Today, you can do something special for yourself. Today you can do something special for someone else. Today, you should do all you can. Tomorrow is not a guarantee. Make today count. May you be blessed beyond your dreams and prayers. Enjoy this day!

October 17:
GOOD MORNING! Welcome to the newest day of your life! So good to have you here today. There may be some tough times in your life. There are also going to be some great times. Those tough times are generally the result of at least one of three possible things. It may be punishment for something you may have done. It

may be God is trying to teach you a lesson. It may also be God is preparing you for something down the road. Either way, the tougher the situation the better most will learn. There is a positive from every negative action. Sometimes you have to look hard. Sometimes it may take a long time to show. Be patient in all things. May this be the greatest day of your life. May you be protected from harm. Appreciate this day for the gift it is.

October 18:
GOOD MORNING! So glad to see you here today. God has plans for you today. It may be answers to prayers. It may be something special you do not know about. It may be another step to something down the road. Just know you are here on purpose and for a reason. You are needed. You are loved. Make the most of every minute of this day. This day is a gift. Fill your life and day with God and positive things and your life will be positive and good. May this be the greatest day of your life. You cannot control what comes at you; however, you can control how you deal with it!

October 19:
GOOD MORNING! No matter how good yesterday was, today can be better. First, let God know you appreciate this day. Then start it with something special and positive. Step outside and listen to the world wake up. Take an early morning walk. Let go of any negative you may have and just appreciate life and the good about it. Let those who are important to you, know you love them. Do everything to the best of your ability. The more positive in your mind; the more positive your life will be. It will make a difference. Reach high for your goals. Make every minute count for something good. This day is a gift. Treat it well!

October 20:
GOOD MORNING! Congratulations, looks like you have been given a new day. You are not going to change the behavior of others, and you should not accept responsibility for the actions of others. The only person you can change is yourself and the only person's actions you are responsible for is yours. Let today be the day you work on yourself. Maybe you feel there is a part of you which could use a little improvement. Be kind to others. Speak to those you pass. Never leave the home angry. Never go to bed angry. Start and end the day with a prayer and everything in between will be better! Appreciate this day and the gift it is.

October 21:
GOOD MORNING! It feels so good to wake up. Your body should be rested or revitalized. Your mind should be clicking with the routine you will attempt to complete today. Maybe, you have the option of what you may want to accomplished today. Whatever you do, today, act like it is the last thing you will do in this world. Put 100% into everything you do. You will feel more complete and content in yourself. Be an inspiration to others. This day is a gift. Have an appreciation for what you have been given. This is your day; now you can get the party started!

October 22:
GOOD MORNING! You are about to be part of a new day. Thank God for the good and easy times. Welcome the lessons that will come your way today. The tougher the lesson, or situation, the more you will learn. The lesson may be a hard one; however, what you learn will be with you forever, if you allow it. At some point, you will need to let go of what you cannot control. Focus on what you have control of. The one thing you have control over is your character. Whether it is good or bad, it is created and maintained by you. May this day bring only good things to you and your loved ones. May you be protected from harm. May you be given wisdom for your decisions and courage to stand alone, if you feel led. This day is a gift. Dwell on the positive and release the negative. You are loved and needed. Life is to short to be unhappy...

October 23:
GOOD MORNING! It is does not matter how bad things were yesterday, you are here today and it is time to let go of your turmoil and issues. You do what you can for others and situations. Then, you just have to let go and move on. You are not responsible for other adult's actions. You also can only help change someone who wants to change. Others have to change themselves. Do not be so quick to criticize others who are acting outside of your expectations. Everyone sins, or does things they should not be doing; whether, it is in thought or actions. In God's eyes, sin is sin, and He will be the judge in the end. Because someone is doing something you do not agree with, does not make them any less a person. Others may be looking at you and thinking the same thing. Let God be the judge and that will be one less concern for you today. Let all your words be kind to others today. Do not pass up the

opportunity to help another. Today is a gift, let every minute count for something good!

October 24:
GOOD MORNING! Congratulations and look what you have. You have a new day, just for you. Your life starts fresh today. If you dwell on yesterday and the past, you will never be happy and slow in moving forward. Let it go. Let yesterday be a lesson and today an adventure. Speak to everyone you meet. You never know when your next good friend is in front of you. Speak kindly of others. You never know who is behind you. Let this be the greatest day of your life. It is all about your attitude. Starting the day with a prayer is a great way to a new beginning! This day is a gift. Enjoy the celebration!

October 25:
GOOD MORNING! Welcome to the newest day of your life. So glad you are here. You will be making decisions today. Sometimes the decisions are easy to make. There will be an obvious benefit, or outcome, which may need to be achieved. Other times, there may not be an obvious, positive, outcome. Those decisions are a lot harder to come to. Sometimes you may have to make a decision when the outcome will be the 'lesser of two evils." Those decisions are usually when you might be called upon to make the "no right or wrong" decisions. Christians usually, will pray when they are in a tough decision making role. Some will recognize a sign or know when God is guiding them. Making those tough decisions are a lot easier when you are listening, or have God in your life. Just because a decision you make is morally, or ethically, the right thing to do, does not mean it was God's plan for you. No one person knows everything. Seek guidance for your tough decisions. The outcome may be much better than shooting from the hip decision. May this a great day for you and your loved ones. May all your prayers and dreams be answered as you asked. Be safe and be blessed. Enjoy the day and make the most of every minute!

October 26:
GOOD MORNING! It appears you have been given a new day. How about making the most of this day? Whatever you do today; do it to the best of your ability. Spend as much time as you can, with your loved ones. Speak kindly to others and let others know

you care. Treat this day as the gift it is. You have this time. You may not have tomorrow. Make it the best day of your life!

October 27:
GOOD MORNING! So it begins. The first day of the rest of your life is here. Congratulations on this great gift. Before using up any of your time with criticisms or judgements; make sure your own house is in order. If negativity is a constant in your life, then, perhaps, something needs to change. You are here to be happy. Help others when you can. Make sure you let those you love, know you love them. You never know what may come to you, at any time. It is better to believe what you see and not so much of what you hear. Make the most of every minute. They are all gifts. You are here for a purpose. Start and end the day with a prayer. Enjoy this day and all it brings. Make it count for something good!

October 28:
GOOD MORNING! It is so good to see you here today. If you knew you were going to be taken from this world and you knew your time was running out, what would you do with your time? Would you spend it huddled in a little ball crying or would you spend it with loved ones, or maybe saying good bye to those you care about, or maybe just sitting and listening to what is around you? The truth is, everyday, you are closing in on your last day in this world. Many will just never know when their job, or purpose, in this world is finished and they will be leaving. Where do you want to spend your next life? In a place described like Hell, or in Heaven? If you have doubts these places exist just take a look around and you will find there are many people who have been to one or the other and in some cases, people have seen both. Give this some thought. You just never know when your time will come. This really is too important to ignore. May this day be a blessing to you and your loved ones. May those who are sick, be healed and those who will pass today, leave this world in peace. Make the most of your time and this day. Now, you can get the party started!

October 29:
GOOD MORNING! Welcome to your new adventure. Throughout your life, others may try to persuade you to do things you are not really comfortable with, or just do not want to do. If you are not comfortable with doing something, there is probably a reason. That is when it is okay to say, "No." God gave you a brain to think

for yourself. Doing something, when you have a feeling it is not right, is going to lead to issues. Whether it be your conscience, or your brain, speaking to you; you are responsible for your own actions. Stand up for yourself. Saying, "No" just may be one of the things you will always be proud of. Make the most of this day. Use your brain, not someone else's. Everyday is a gift. Make the most of this one. The clock is ticking!

October 30:
GOOD MORNING! Your presence really does make this day better. No matter where you are, or what you doing, you are loved, thought of, and missed. There are others who would give anything to hear kind words from you. Others would give anything to see a smile from you. Reach out and touch as many as you can today. Let them know you care and love them. Take advantage of the time you are alone and thank God for who you are and what you have. Give to others who are not so blessed. You have the power to give others a reason to be happy. That is always a good thing. May this be the greatest day of your life and may all your dreams and prayers come true. You make this day special!

October 31:
GOOD MORNING! Welcome to your newest day. It is so easy to get all tangled up in what is going on in your day. There may be health issues, personal issues in the family, or financial concerns. Sometimes, it is good to just take a step back and look at who is in your life and what miracles are happening everyday around you. It is those brief moments which may help keep you planted in how good life really is. If you ever feel your cup is running over, remember, someone else has been there before and survived. Whatever you are going through is temporary and there are others who would give anything to trade places with you. Let this be the greatest day of your life. Understand the most important things in your life are those which you cannot put a price on!

November 1:
GOOD MORNING! The new day is here and you have arrived. Since you have been given this new day, you may as well make the most of every minute and enjoy the whole thing. Smile at the little hurdle's and issues. Share the good times and enjoy the moments with others. Take those opportunities to help others. Let those who are special to you, know you care.Take the time to listen to others. Start the day with a prayer for guidance and thanks. End the day with a prayer of gratitude. That makes everything in between better. This is your day. Make it a good day. Go ahead and get your party started!

November 2:
GOOD MORNING! It is a great feeling knowing you are here today and you have been given another day in this world. When you woke up this morning, did you consider how blessed you are? Today, many already have plans for their day. Many will have the option of doing what they want. Whatever it is you do; do it with 100% of your capabilities, and with a smile. Speak to those you pass and get to know others. There are some great people out there and a smile from you may be just what someone needs to turn their day around. There are people who wish they could be doing what you may be doing today. Make the most of this day and share your happiness with others! Get on out there and see what positive things you can do!

November 3:
GOOD MORNING! It is a new day and it feels so good. Yesterday, is in the past and there may have been some lessons learned. Today should be all about the positive things going on. The more positive feelings you have; the more positive your life will be. If others are coming against you in some way, ignore them. People who deceive others to get their way, are busy digging their own hole. Do not waste your time being vindictive. Spend your time in positive ways doing good things. It is, almost, comical when people get their way sometimes. They have no idea what they bring upon themselves. May this be a day of peace for you and your loved ones. Appreciate the time with your loved ones and let others know you care. Never leave your house or go to bed angry. May this be the greatest day of your life and may you be blessed beyond your dreams and prayers. This is your day, go get it!

November 4:
GOOD MORNING! And, so it begins. This would be the newest day of your life and the first day of the rest of your life. Welcome this day and all it brings. When you have more than you really need; a person may become unappreciative and begin to take things for granted. Then a person may come to expect things rather than appreciating what they have. Once people come to the point of expecting things; they may become disappointed if they do not get their way or what they want. Disappointment brings negative feelings and then possible negative behavior. That is how easy it is for negativity to crawl into your life. Appreciate what you have. Work for what you want. Material things are appreciated more when they have to be earned. Positive emotions are also appreciated more when they are earned. Start this day right and appreciate being here. God has a purpose for you. Let Him into your life. Do not be afraid. May this be a special day for you and your loved ones. May you be safe and protected. Go ahead and get your party started!

November 5:
GOOD MORNING! The sun comes up another day in your life. No matter what happened yesterday; today is a new day, and it is time to appreciate, enjoy and make the most of it. Start and end your day with a prayer. Be kind to those you speak with. Let others know you care. Let go of the negative thoughts and feelings. Fill your day with the positive and you will be much happier. Forgiving others for pain they may have caused may be hard. Not forgiving them is allowing them to hurt you over and over and is a waste of your time and energy. May you and your loved ones be protected from harm. May you be given the opportunity to help others and may this be the greatest day of your life!

November 6:
GOOD MORNING! Today is the start of the rest of your life. Let go of the negative. Fill the void which is left with positive thoughts, feelings and actions. If you can do just one small positive thing for someone today; which you, and they will remember forever. That makes this a great day. If you can do one small thing positive thing, everyday, for someone else, you will have a great life and feel good about yourself and others. Today is the day to start. May this be the greatest day of your life. May your prayers be answered and your faith strong. May you also be protected from harm. This

is the first day of the rest of your life. Make it count for something special!

November 7:
GOOD MORNING! It appears you have been blessed with a new day. This day is a gift from God and should be used wisely. There are others who look to you for support, love, attention, and guidance. You are important in this world. You are loved and needed in this world. You also have a special purpose in this world. You will know you have found the purpose of your life by the feeling of wholeness you will have. You are too valuable and special to waste a single minute. Make every minute count for something. In the end, you will find there are not many of those minutes. Smile and speak to those you pass. Reach out to those who need help. This day is a gift. Appreciate it. Make it the best day you can!

November 8:
GOOD MORNING! So glad to see you here today. You owe it to yourself to make the best of this day. God does want you to be happy and content in your life. If you are not, you may be going through a lesson he has thrown your way. It may be because of decisions you have made. A good way to start your day is having an appreciation for life itself. Step outside and watch as the sun lights the sky in the east for a few days. You may not be able to see the sun rise on the horizon; however you can see it light up the sky. Look at the grass, the trees and all around you which breathes and has life. There are miracles all around you. Have an appreciation for life and all that is in your life. Your life could change in the wink of an eye today. Make the most of every minute. May you be blessed with good health, wisdom and guidance. The day is already moving. This day is a gift and it is time to get the party started!

November 9:
GOOD MORNING: It is great to see you having another day. It would be an even greater feeling to know you are fed, warm and in a loving environment. Many have that everyday. Many have all that on some days. There are some who have all that on very few days. Some are lacking the basics of life, through no fault of their own. Some do not feel good about themselves and do not feel they deserve to have good things. Some do not even feel good enough about themselves to allow the basics. Some feel that way because they might not have been treated well at a critical time in their

lives. Some may have done something which has always bothered them and they have been punishing themselves. Sometimes, it does not take much to turn someone's day around, if not their life. Just a few moments of your time may give someone all the encouragement they need to feel good about themselves. There is nothing wrong with asking a person, who looks like they are in desperation, if they are ok, or if you can help them. There is something wrong with walking past someone who is in need and not speaking to them. It is by the Grace of God you are not in their shoes. One day you may be. Do one good thing for a person today and expect nothing in return. That will make this a great day! May you and your loved ones be blessed with protection and good health. Make this a great day.

November 10:

GOOD MORNING: It is so good to see you are here today. Great things may happening for you today. Waking up is a great thing and a good way to start this day. Working on your spirituality, as well as your attitude towards life and the lives of others, is very important. Taking care of your body is also very important. It is more important to eat right and get the exercise you need before you get sick; rather than, waiting until you get sick. Take care of yourself. You are important and people need you in this world. Life is short enough. Do not shorten it by being a couch potato and eating whatever is in a bag. Take a walk and take the time to fix some healthy food. It is not that hard and you may be glad you did later. This day is a gift. Make it count for something good!

November 11:

GOOD MORNING! Thank you for being here today. Your presence makes this day better. Like the sun rises and sets, your issues will come and go. It is not the issue that makes things good or bad. It is all about your attitude. Car did not start this morning? Maybe that was God keeping you from an accident. Loose a loved during the night. Maybe, God is reminding you we all will pass from this world and you need to appreciate and make the best use of the time you have with others before they leave. Look for your purpose in this world. You are here for a reason. Ask for wisdom for your decisions. May you and your loved ones be healthy and protected from harm. May this be the greatest day of your life!

November 12:
GOOD MORNING! So, a new day begins for you. Maybe today is a good day to pay more attention to the actions of those around you; rather, than the words they may be speaking. There can be a great deal of difference in what someone says and what someone does. Sometimes it is intentional, sometimes not. Either way, following others is not always a good thing. Many seem to have their own ulterior motives, as their priority, these days. If something is bothering you about a situation, there is probably a reason. You are responsible for your own actions. You are not responsible for the actions of others. May this day flow smoothly and may there be only good things in your path. May you and your loved ones be blessed. Smile and speak to those you pass and never pass on an opportunity to help someone! This day is a gift. Make it a good one!

November 13:
GOOD MORNING! Since you are going to be here (congratulations, by the way) you may as well make this the best day you can. Since you want to make it a special day, you will need to do something special; whether it be for yourself, or someone else. Maybe you can make this the first day of a new life attitude change. Let your loved ones know you love them. Let go of and leave the negative behind you. Speak only kind words to and of others. Dump any anger you are carrying around. Forget about being vindictive. Everyone has an opinion. Usually it is better to wait and be asked, before giving it. Be generous to others; whether you know them or not. Know you are not perfect, and neither is anyone else. Seek guidance and wisdom from the right places. Have an appreciation for all that you have. Above all, start and end your day with a prayer. This day really is a gift. Treat it as best you can. Now, you can get your party started!

November 14:
GOOD MORNING! A new day has been given to you. Sooner or later in your life, you will have a situation develop which you will have no control over. It may be a situation which you did, or did not, create. It may be health. It may be a medical issue. It may be financial. There may be "professionals" who can help you through that time. They may be a doctor, lawyer, counselor, or some other "professional." You may feel you need more than just a "professional." This is when people will reach out and pray. Do not wait until you need God, to speak to Him. God already knows you. God

also knows you are not perfect. Talk to him in the good times as well as the bad. God has given you this day for a reason. He has a purpose for your life. If you have not found it yet, keep your eyes and ears open. It will come. May this be the greatest day of your life. May you, and your loved ones be protected from harm. May your mind be sharp and may you be blessed with wisdom. Today is a gift. Enjoy all of and every minute of it. You are not guaranteed tomorrow.

November 15:
GOOD MORNING! Glad you are able to be here today. Today should be a day to focus on the things you can change and make happen. Things which you are able to control and be responsible for. Let the other stuff: the drama, the speculations, and the rumors go away. You cannot control others, so why spend your time trying? Fill your day and life with positive and the joy will follow. You can control your attitude and make this day better, no matter what comes your way. Remember to let your loved ones know you care; before anyone leaves the home today. Start and end the day with a prayer. That can make all the difference in the world. Do not wait until you need God to speak to Him and expect things to happen.. Thank Him for the day. May this be a blessed day for you! You already have a great start!

November 16:
GOOD MORNING! Welcome the first day of the rest of your life. Have you planned something special so you can remember this day? Today may be a great day to take some time and spend it with your loved ones. Take a walk, watch a movie, go to the zoo, bake a cake, make some ice cream sundaes, and pray together are all things that can provide great memories. This is a great day to bring out the Bible and share some reading. Do something "out of the box." Make this day count for something. Today is a blessing and tomorrow you may not have the opportunities you have today. Enjoy every minute of this gift and make the most of it! Go ahead and get your party started!

November 17:
GOOD MORNING! It appears you have arrived at your new day. This day and time has been aside just for you. This day is yours. The only request is you must make the most of this day because tomorrow is not a guarantee. Be patient in your wants and desires.

Pray often and help those you can. Never leave your home and never go to bed angry. You are in this world to be happy. If you are not, change your life. No one is going to make you happy. That is an emotion which comes from yourself. May this be the greatest day of your life. May you be safe and protected. May you have the guidance and wisdom for the decisions you will need to make. This is your day. Go get it

November 18:
GOOD MORNING! Welcome to the first day of the rest of your life. If you were to leave this world today, how will you be remembered? It is up to you if there will be good thoughts about your life. It is up to you if your memories will be of someone who did for others. It is going to be up to you if you are missed or just left a name. Make this day count for something good. Leave something good in your wake. May this be a great day for you and your loved ones. Be kind in your words and patient with others. Be forgiving towards others. Be the best you can be at whatever you do. This day is a gift. Get your party started and enjoy it like there is no tomorrow!

November 19:
GOOD MORNING! It is a new day, not just another day! You may open this day like you might a gift. You can tear into it, or peel the paper away slowly. Either way, take the time to make the most of it and enjoy the day as the gift it is. Feeling like you are better than others, just makes your inevitable fall hurt more. God has given you a special ability. When you find that ability you may also find God's purpose for you in this world. Today is going to be a great day. Sometimes, it takes a little longer to see the greatness in it. May this be the greatest day of your life. May you and your family be protected from harm. May your heart be filled with the joy you were meant to have. This day is a gift. Take great care of it and appreciate it.

November 20:
GOOD MORNING! Welcome to the newest day of your life. Seeking guidance for some decisions is a wise thing to do. Even the most intelligent people, seek guidance. No one knows everything. Seek your guidance from someone who has been faced with your same situation. Those who believe in God will seek their guidance from God, through prayer. He will always show you the best way.

It may not be in your time. It is all about your faith. Start your day with a prayer. Be thankful for who you are and what you have been given. You are special. You are loved and you are needed in this world. There is a special purpose for you to be here today. This day is God's first gift to you today. Make the most of this day and let the issues from yesterday stay in the past. Move forward. Be blessed and speak kindly to and of others. Today is really a gift. Enjoy it and now, go ahead and get your party started!

November 21:
GOOD MORNING! You may have something going on in your life which is holding you down and keeping you from having the happiness in your life you were meant to have. You are going to have to deal with negative situations; which, may involve people you have no control over. There are people who have been in your situation before and they survived, as you will. Whatever you are dealing with; it will come to an end. You will have to come to a point and accept that you have done everything you can. You do the best you can with these situations, then let them go. May today be the day you are able to let "it" go. Move forward with your life and do not allow issues to hold you back any longer. May the arms of God protect you and keep you and your loved ones from harm, Start and end this day with a prayer and everything in between will be much easier. Today is a gift. Enjoy it and use it to the best of your ability.

November 22:
GOOD MORNING! It is so good to see you are here today. People will remember you for some small act of kindness you did for them, or someone else, for many years. People may also remember an act of cruelty you showed to another. How do you want to be remembered? Do you consider your words before responding to an emotional situation? Do you pass a person on the street, who might appear to need some type of help, without speaking? Are you grateful for everyday you have in this world? A good attitude will make your day so much better and your life so much happier. Being happy comes from within yourself. Sometimes, you may forget just how special you are in this world. There are people who love you, people who want and need you in their lives, along with the people whose days are made special by the sound of your voice. During your lifetime you will leave memories with many. Those memories will be a direct result of your actions and attitude.

A good attitude will make your day so much better and your life so much happier. It will also effect those around you in a positive way. Count your blessings at the beginning of every day. Blessings begin with the things you cannot buy. You have been given life today. Your blessings started when you awoke. Make the most of every minute and share your happiness with others. Leave at least one special memory in your path today. Today is a gift. Now enjoy it!

November 23:
GOOD MORNING! Considering this is the first day of the rest of your life; you can call it the best day of your life. Congratulations on this great gift you have been given. Be grateful for what you have and who you have in your life. Everyone is responsible to someone. Eventually, you will be accountable for all you have done in your life. You may want to keep this in mind as you go through your day and the rest of your life. Help others when given the opportunity. Start and end your day with a prayer. This make everything in between so much easier or better! This day is a gift. Make the most of every minute and thank God for it!

November 24:
GOOD MORNING! Welcome and congratulations on your new day. Have you experienced a recent situation which has caused you to question your faith in yourself? There is a lot of that going on. Many are suffering from financial situations and other situations which they have not brought about on their own.   There are a lot of outside influences in our lives. Sometimes you may be able to dodge the harmful ones. Sometimes, you may not even see them coming. Chances are good your ability to make decisions has not changed from last week until today. Do not let a bad situation drag you into doubting yourself. Deal with your situation, then stand up, and move into a direction to reach whatever goal you have set for yourself. You may have to change your direction to reach that goal. Just keep moving forward. God has given everyone the strength to deal with the situations they have to deal with. Sometimes you just have to dig a little deeper. Today is going to be a great day for you. It is up to you just how good it will be. Go ahead and get your party started!

November 25:
GOOD MORNING! The newest day of your life has begun. If you have not said, "Thank you" for this day then now is a good time. It is a good day to be alive. Be grateful for the day; no matter what kind of issues you have to deal with. You make the world a much more pleasant place and you still have a job, or purpose, in being here. Keep in mind, there are many who would give anything just to be in your shoes and live your life. There are many needing help out there. Never pass up an opportunity to help another. You just never know how much one act of kindness may change someone's life. May God keep you and your loved ones from harm. May God also keep you strong and give you guidance for your decisions. Do not allow yourself to be pulled in others' drama or chaos. This is your day and all that you can make of it is yours. Go ahead and get your party started!

November 26:
GOOD MORNING! So good to see you here today. You make the day much better. Your presence completes the day for many others too. There would be a hole in the world without your presence. The size of that hole will depend on you and what you do during your time here. People depend on you as you depend on others. There are people who need to hear your voice today. There are people who need to know you are there for them. There is someone who you need to hear from. There is someone there for you, when you need them. Appreciate those relationships. Some are going to be very special and long lasting. Some may be short and stay in your mind forever. Get to know those you meet. You just never know who you may speaking to. Appreciate this day and all it brings also. Everything that happens is either a blessing or a lesson. Breathe deeply, smile and let others know you care as you go through the day. You are as good as you give. May this be the most blessed day of your life. Take advantage of what God has given you. Maybe today will be the day you learn what the special purpose in your life is, if you do not yet. This day is a gift. Now, it is up to you what you make of it...

NOVEMBER 27:
GOOD MORNING! Your new day has arrived and begun. Turn your back on the darkness you may have faced yesterday and walk into the light of this gift of a new day. Your life starts now and it starts fresh. No matter what happened yesterday, today starts the

first day of the rest of your life. Do not allow yourself to be led into a world of deceit, chaos or instability. This is your life. You are responsible for your actions and behavior. Make the most of every minute of this day. Enjoy what you have and who you have in your life. Life is not always going to be easy. It is also too precious not to enjoy. Start and end the day with a prayer. That makes everything in between much better. May this be the most blessed day of your life. May you and your family have the protection of God and wisdom of his guidance. This is your day.

November 28:
GOOD MORNING! It is a great day to be alive. Yesterday was one less day in your life; which means, your life is shorter by one day. It is good to do good things for others in this world. Hurting others is not so good; whether, it be financially, mentally, or physically. There is a price for your actions. Man's law punishes in this world. There is also the punishment some call "karma." Christians call that, "God speaking or God's lesson." Everyone makes mistakes and does things they might regret or know they should not do. No one is perfect. If you knew you would be going to another world from this one and you knew you would have to answer for your "indiscretions"; what would your attitude be then? May this be a good day for you and your loved ones. May your eyes be open and may your heart be filled with the joy it was meant to have. May you also have wisdom for your decisions. Let this be a great day!

November 29:
GOOD MORNING! A new day begins. More of life adventures may come your way today. Some of those adventures will be opportunities to learn and some will be opportunities to move you closer to goals. Opportunities have a tendency of coming to busy people. The busier you are; the more opportunities you will have. The more opportunities you have the busier you become. May today a day of opportunities. May today be a great day for you and your loved ones. May your day be filled with the joy and happiness you were meant to have. This day is a gift. Take advantage of today's first opportunity and go get it!

November 30:
GOOD MORNING! So, you have a new day. There are not too many things, of life, more relaxing than watching the sun come up on the horizon. It does not have to rise over a body of water to be

beautiful. It could rise over your neighbors home. There is something special about the world lighting up and warming up everyday. It is a few moments when you can realize how blessed you are to be here and what a miracle life is. It is also, usually, one of the quiet parts of your day. Make the most of your day, just as you would the brief few minutes of a sun rise. Appreciate being here and those you are here with. You are here for such a short time. May this be a day of appreciation and celebration of all you have been given. Enjoy every minute and make the most of your time. Enjoy this gift!

December 1:
GOOD MORNING! It is good to see you have this day; to share yourself with the world. People are looking forward to seeing you and hearing from you today. Others want to enjoy your company. It may not always seem like it. You are very important to others in this world. Whether good or bad, you have done things in the past, even years ago, which others still remember. You may not have seen someone for years and yet they can still remember an action you were involved with. You may have effected the lives of many from your past. You may effect the lives of many others in your future. Let those actions and effects be positive. Think before speaking and may your words always be kind and positive. IT is really good to see you here today!

December 2:
GOOD MORNING! It appears you have a new day in your life. It is up to you what you can accomplish today. A happy person does not begin the day by dreading it. You are only being held back by the negative thoughts you are carrying. Think about how great life is without the negative thoughts and feelings from the past and present. Think about how great life is when your days are filled with only positive thoughts and emotions. God has given you this day. God also wants you to be happy and your heart filled with joy. God also gives you the ability to have this happiness. If being happy escapes you; then maybe, you are traveling down the wrong road and you may need a change. Start your day with a prayer. Thank God for this day and all the blessings you have around you. Without appreciation for what you have, you have nothing. May this be the greatest day of your life. May you touch the lives of others and may your heart be filled with the joy it was meant to have! Now, get your party started!

December 3:
GOOD MORNING! A new day has started and you are to be in it! You may know of someone who is in total despair. It may be about a decision they dread, or a decision they need to make; which has no obvious positive outcome. There are going to be those decisions and events in our lives. These are life lessons. The stress from making the decision may be blinding you, or someone you know. There is, usually, a positive outcome for every negative action. Sometimes, it may take a while to see the positive; however, you will see it, if you allow yourself to. Always, seek advice for your de-

cisions. Seek that advice from someone who has been in your shoes before. Not everyone has been where you are so be selective about where you get your advice. Christians will pray about their decisions. God may not give you the answer right away. Be patient. Sometimes God has something else planned for you and it may take a little more time. People have a tendency of being afraid of the unknown. Educate yourself, seek guidance and then act. Sometimes there are no right or wrong decisions. Maybe, just the lesser of two evils will be the choice. Have faith in yourself and move on once you have acted. Whatever the decision or issue is; life is too short to dwell on it. May you be blessed beyond your desires and prayers. May you and your loved ones be protected from harm. May this be the greatest day of your life! Today is a gift!

December 4:
GOOD MORNING! It's a glorious new day to enjoy and share! Since you are going to be here; you should make the most of it! Spend some time with your loved ones. Do something different with those you care about. Have some ice cream, sit outside, walk in the rain, or maybe just sit and think about the blessings you had in your life. You do not have to have anyone else with you to do something different. Do something which brings peace to you. The point of doing this, is to remember those few moments long from now. Anytime, you get stressed, remember that time and let yourself go back to the peace you had. May this be the greatest day of your life. May you be at peace with all that is around you. May you respect and love yourself. May you have good health and be wise in your decisions. This day is a gift. Now, you can get your party started!

December 5:
GOOD MORNING! Welcome to the latest and newest day of your life. You have been made a part of this day because you are special. You have a special purpose in being here. You are a segment of a much larger picture of this world. Even though you are a small segment of this world you will have a great effect. Your presence will effect others. It may be family, friends or colleagues. You will effect others in small ways and, in some cases, you may effect others for life. Others will be listening to your words and watching your actions. Some will look to you because they trust you. Some will look to you for advice. Some will look to you when times are tough; whether it be financial, emotional, or just someone to talk

with. Be kind in your words. Be patient with others. You never know how someone is feeling unless you have been in their shoes before. Life's events effects everyone differently. Someone may be at their wits end and just need to vent. Others may be looking for advice. Cutting someone off without listening may be devastating to some. Your words can change others worlds. Treat others as you would want to be treated or better. You will feel good about it and you will live without regrets. May your heart be filled with the joy it was meant to have. May you be at peace with yourself and others. Do not be in rush to get to the next day. Every minute gone by is one less minute in the world. Make the most of every one! Share the joy of your world with others. This day is a gift. Thank God for it!

December 6:
GOOD MORNING! Well, you have arrived at the first day of the rest of your life. This day has been given to you, and for you, by God. He is the one who will be beside you when everyone has gone home. He is the one who will carry you through the tough times. He is the one who will protect you from harm. He is the one everyone will turn to when they have done all they can do. He is the one who loves you so much, he allowed his own son, Jesus, to die for you. He does all this and all he asks is that you do not reject him and believe in him and his son. He is the only one who will keep you from a lifetime in hell when you pass to your next life. If you believe in Heaven, then you have to believe in hell. Why take a chance where you spend your next life? If you have not talked with God, today is a good day to do that. Do not wait until it is too late and your time is up. God can change your life and make everything much brighter around you! Enjoy your day. Make the most of every minute. Every minute is a gift. May this be the most blessed day of your life!

December 7:
GOOD MORNING! Your day has already started off well, just by waking up. So glad to see you have another day in this world. This world functions much better with you in it. Just knowing you are here provides happiness and security to others. You do have a special reason, or purpose, in being here. Some will effect many, many lives. Some will effect only a few. You are here to effect others lives in a positive way. The decision to do that is yours. Some will be given the opportunity to help and yet; they will not take

that opportunity. The situation may be a very small thing to you. It may be everything to someone else. Never pass up an opportunity to help another. You just never know what that will mean or the effect that will have on someone else and their life. Be kind in your words. Think before you respond in anger. You will not be able to take the words back once they come out. The wrong word, or words can damage others and yourself for life. May this be the greatest day of your life. May you have more than you pray for and may you be protected from harm and be given wisdom for your decisions. This day is a gift. Make the most of every minute and make them count for something good and positive. Go get it!

December 8:
GOOD MORNING! Congratulations and welcome to the newest day of your life! So glad you are here and there are others who will be glad to see you here too. Today is a good day to let go of all that may be troubling you. Worrying takes a lot out of a person. It uses up energy you could be using on positive things. The space worrying uses in your mind and body, is draining on your system. Worrying ages a person and can actually change your personality. Sometimes bad things happen to good people. That is just the way it is. Learn from those times. Do not spend your day worrying about things you have no control over. Say a prayer and move on! Enjoy the time you have with loved ones or spend some quality time on your own. Do something you want to do. Today is a gift for you. Never leave the house or go to bed angry. Make the most of every minute of your day. Go ahead and get your party started!

December 9:
GOOD MORNING! So, the first day of the rest of your life begins. It is good to know you will be a part of this day. Today is a great day to do one small, special something for someone. Do not expect anything in return. They do not even have to know you did that one small, special something. You might be amazed at what a good feeling that one small act gives. You may even want to do it again! Speak to those you pass. Let go of any anger or vindictiveness you may be carrying. Be selective of your friends. This is a great day for you to be you. You are loved just the way you are. This day is a gift. Appreciate every minute you have. Go ahead and enjoy this day. It is brought to you by God.

December 10:

GOOD MORNING! Being happy is not always an easy emotion to have. There are times when the actions or words, of others, will hurt you. There are times when you may be disappointed about the outcome of a situation. There are times when, even in a room full of people, you may feel alone. Sometimes the actions of others, or their words will reveal their true self. Words or actions will only hurt as long as you allow them too. Your self respect should dictate whether you will allow yourself to be around others who may hurt you, or not. The outcome of situations will not always be what you had hoped, or prayed for. When a door closes on a situation another opportunity will arise. It may be better, so do not allow a disappointment to effect your day in a negative way. Chances are good, that disappointment will be forgotten later in life. Something bigger and better may be just around the corner. When you feel alone, take the opportunity to thank God for the blessings you have. That is a great time to do a self evaluation and see where you are heading and what you may want to change in your life. Know the difference in being alone and being lonely. If you are feeling lonely, that may be the perfect time to do something you have wanted to do and have not done. You do not have to check with others so take advantage of that time. You may want to go out and help someone who needs some help. You have made this day so much better. Thank you for being here and share yourself with others. There are many who look forward to hearing, or seeing you. May this be the greatest day of you life. Today is a gift, now get your party started!

December 11:

GOOD MORNING! Congratulations on the newest day in the journey of life. May you be blessed beyond your dreams and prayers. May your health be good and your decisions be made with guidance and wisdom. Tomorrow is not guaranteed, so make the most of every minute of today. If you settle for less than you wanted, you may never be satisfied or know the happiness you were meant to have. May this be the greatest day of your life. May you be remembered for the good things you do today! Start and end this day with a prayer and everything in between will be much better. This day is yours. Enjoy it!

December 12:

GOOD MORNING! It appears that you have another day, brought to you by God. Start it off right with a little prayer and be appreciative of what you have in your life. Think only positive thoughts and push negative thoughts out of your mind. Let go of the issues from yesterday and focus in on today. Do not concern yourself with tomorrow's issues. Do everything to the best of your ability; no matter how small. Smile and speak to everyone you pass. Never pass someone in need. Do everything in moderation. Read at least one verse from the Bible and talk to God often. Let those you love, know your feelings. This is your day. It is precious and will only come once in your life. Make the most of it. Now, go ahead and get your party started!

December 13:

GOOD MORNING! Welcome to what may be the greatest day of your life. Today, may be the day to open doors you have been procrastinating about. Today, may be the day you let others know you are not here to be taken advantage of. Today, may be the day you let animosity, from the past, go. Today, may be the day you realize anger will not change events in your life. Today, may be the day you realize it is easier to smile, than frown. Today, may be the day you find your purpose in this world. Today, may be the day you really appreciate your life! Today is your day. Go get it and make it the best you can!

December 14:

GOOD MORNING! A new day has arrived. You are invited to enjoy all it has to offer. Leave yesterday in the past and step into the first day of the rest of your life. Today may not be perfect; however, very few things are. What is perfect? Your body is designed to operate perfectly. Your heart, which seemingly pumps forever and has the ability to pump blood which carries oxygen for your brain and muscles is designed perfectly. The lungs which take in one kind of gas and releases a harmful gas is designed perfectly. Your digestive tract which takes in food and changes it into energy for your body is designed perfectly. Your bone structure and all the connecting tissues which allow you to walk, run, hold and move things is designed perfectly. All of this working together, with your brain, is perfectly designed. Designed, not created by accident or randomness. You are a miracle. Your presence was designed. You are here for a reason. You are here to effect other's lives in some positive way. Maybe today is the day you find that special purpose. Never let an opportunity to help another go by. Listen more than you speak. That is the way to learn. God does not make mistakes. You are important and you are needed. You were designed. May this be a very special and blessed day for you. May your heart and mind be opened to what God has planned for you. Today is your gift. Enjoy it and get your party started!

December 15:
GOOD MORNING: Let today be a day of peace and happiness. Avoid the drama around you. Give everything your best and leave yesterday in the past. Life is good! Start and end your day with a prayer..It will make everything in between much better..May this be the greatest day of your life and may you and your loved ones be blessed. This day is a gift..Enjoy it!

December 16:
GOOD MORNING! The newest day has arrived and it looks like you are to be a part of it. Just as your body changes, your spirit and soul will also change daily. Just as your physical body adjusts to what it eats and drinks, your mind, soul and spirit will change with what you hear, see and do. Unhealthy foods will damage your body. Unhealthy thoughts and environments will damage your personality, your soul and your spirit. Surrounding yourself with positive people, behavior, and actions will give you a positive outlook which will also lead to more pleasant personality. If you actions are always positive then you will be able to look forward and be someone others want to be around. You will also be happy in your life and may find your purpose in this world sooner. Negative actions towards others will always be in the back of your mind and admit it or not, your mind will always be occupied with the consequences of that action. Let this be a positive day. Help others when you have that opportunity. Smile and speak to all those you pass. Get to know the others in your world. Never leave your home or go to bed angry. May all your words always be kind. You never know when the last words you speak to someone may, indeed, be the last words you speak to someone. You want to remember those words as being good. Start and end your day with a prayer. Meeting God may come to you at anytime of the day. Enjoy this day as the gift it is. Make the most of every minute of the day. Today is your gift, from God. Now, get your party started!

December 17:
GOOD MORNING! Glad you are able to attend this newest day. The door has opened and you can just step right on in. Please remove your shoes and all the stuff you may have stepped in yesterday, behind. There is only limited time to be here so you want to have a clean start. Due to the limited amount of time today you will be required to enjoy every minute. That means a lot of smiling and speaking to others. Get to know those around you. Not everyone you meet will be worthy of your friendship; however, many will be. You do not want to miss any good ones. The day is best started with appreciation and gratitude for being here. The best way to do that is with a prayer. Keep your eyes open to the opportunities which may come your way today. Listen more than you speak. May all your prayers be answered. May your health be good. May your heart be filled with the joy it was meant to have. This day is a gift. Thank God for it and enjoy it!

December 18:
GOOD MORNING! It appears you hold a special part in a new day. Today, things may not be perfect for you. Today, things may not go well for you. Today, you may not have all you want. Today, you may not be able to do all that you would like. Today, you may be in a situation you do not want to be in. Well, tomorrow things may be perfect for you. Tomorrow, things may go just the way you planned. Tomorrow, you may be able to do all the things you wanted to do. Tomorrow, your situation may be different. Not everyday is going to be perfect. If everyday was perfect you would not have an appreciation for the really good days. This day is still a gift. Make the most of every moment and enjoy all the moments you may have here. Everything which happens, is either a lesson or a blessing. May you get as you give and may God bless you and those of your home. Enjoy this gift. Life is the most precious of all gifts.

December 19:
GOOD MORNING! You have a new day. Life is not always going to be easy. There will be many successes and disappointments. It is how you handle the successes and disappointments which is most important. You may want to thank God for the successes before celebrating. You may want to look at the lesson(s) you can learn with disappointments. Never give up on your goals. Keep moving forward in your life. Do not allow yourself to become stagnant. If

plan "A" does not seem to be working, switch to plan "B". Just make sure the benefits warrant the time and effort involved. Just because you "want" something, does not always mean it is good, or meant, for you. The longer you dwell on one of life's disappointments, the harder it will be to move forward. Let go and move on. Your time is too valuable to waste. You are only here for a short period of time. Make this a great day for yourself and those around you. Share your smile and joy with others. Let others know you care. Go ahead and get this day started!

December 20:
GOOD MORNING! Welcome to your newest day. This day has special activities planned, just for you. People may want to see you. People may want to hear your voice and talk with you. There is so much to do; yet, you will have only a short period of time to get all you can, done. You may have to choose between what others want or what you would like to do. You may have to choose between sharing yourself with older people or younger people. You may have to choose between friends or family. You may have to choose between working or playing. You may have to choose between staying home or going somewhere. You may have to choose between reading a book, taking a walk, writing a letter, cooking something special, or just sitting and thanking God for all the blessings you have in your life. Do not let the negativity of others or the world effect your day. This day is a gift with a time limit. Make it count for all you can. This day is special. Go ahead and get your party started!

December 21:
GOOD MORNING! It is good to know, the sun is coming up for you today. You do not have to respond to negativity which may come your way today. Usually, it is better to turn and walk away. Whether, it is verbal or in action, negativity is not good for you. You will never know your full potential if negativity is a part of, or controlling your life. Becoming angry, is a waste of your time and energy. Move on to better things. You were given this day to learn and have a heart full of happiness; while helping others. Sadly, not everyone will return home today. Make the most of your day because you never know when your time to leave this world will come. It may come in the blink of an eye. Believe in God, and let him know you love him as he loves you. He will give you peace in the worst of situations. May you be protected from harm and

blessed beyond your prayers. May this be the greatest day of your life! Today, is a gift, make it count for something good!

December 22:
GOOD MORNING! It is a great day to be alive. It is also a great day to be you. There are people who would like to be you. You were made special, for a special purpose in this world. If you have not found that special purpose, today may be the day you find out what God has planned for you. You effect people's lives almost everyday. There will come a time when you effect other's lives in a great way. It may be one person. It may be more than one. The effect may not even be significant while you are in this world. This purpose could come as a result of someone you helped at one time. It may be the result of some work you accomplished. It may come as a result of the way you respond to someone, at one time or another. You may even be the reason someone is able to find a true cure for many of today's diseases. The reason, or purpose, for you being here is endless. You are very important in this world. Do your best, be your best and your effect will be it's best. Let this be the greatest day of your life. May you be protected from harm, blessed with good health and may your prayers be answered. This day is a gift and you will only get what you put into it. The world is blessed to have you in it! Live every minute as the most important minute of your life. Go ahead and get your party started!

December 23:
GOOD MORNING! You have been given the gift of a new day. Let this day be a great day for yourself. Smile and speak to those you pass. Help others when you can. Do not allow other's words to have a negative impact in your day. You do not have to be perfect. Make the most of every minute. You never know when your reason, or purpose, in this world may be finished and you are moved to the next world. You make this day special!

December 24:
GOOD MORNING! May this be a day of peace for you and your loved ones. May only happiness flood your hearts and minds. May your prayers be answered and may your love influence others. Your presence makes this day special. Enjoy the gift of today.

December 25:
GOOD MORNING! May today be the day you understand what is truly important in this world. May you and your loved ones know happiness and contentment. Let this be a day of appreciation and joy. The sun has come up for you again this day. Make the most of every minute and continue looking forward! May God bless you and your loved ones on this special day!

December 26:
GOOD MORNING! It does not matter what is going on in your life; you are blessed. Have an appreciation for what you have. Have an appreciation for those in your life; past and present. They are not replaceable. It is the smaller things in life that will count. Do not wait until you lose the important things to recognize what brings you happiness. Enjoy today and everyday. Help others when you can. Life is short. Do your best at everything you do. Today is a gift. Make the most of every minute. Go ahead get your party started!

December 27:
GOOD MORNING! Today is a great day to double check your list of goals and see if you are still on track. It is also a good day to check and make sure your priorities are correct. Look at what, or who, is most important in your life. If you were to leave this world today; will you be remembered as someone who was kind or hurt others? Start and end your day with a prayer. It will make everything in between, easier. May you be protected from harm and given wisdom for your decisions. May this be the most blessed day of your life!

December 28:
GOOD MORNING! This will be the newest day of your life. The choices you make today, are up to you. The decisions you make are up to you. There are positive and negative consequences for all of our actions and decisions. Things are not always going to happen as you hoped, wished, or prayed. No one is perfect. Mistakes will be made. If you do not seek wisdom and guidance for some of your decisions; there may be more negative than positive outcomes. Where you seek your guidance is just as important as actually seeking guidance and wisdom. Everyone needs guidance sooner or later. Asking for guidance may be a lot better than the consequences which may follow without wisdom. May you be protected

from harm. May your decisions be with guidance and wisdom. May peace be in your heart and mind today.

December 29:
GOOD MORNING! Welcome to the first day of the rest of your life. It does not matter what you dealt with yesterday. It does not matter what someone did to you yesterday. It does not matter who said what about you. Today is a gift. Today is your new day. It is better than a new toy. It is better than any new material item. It is a new start on your life. There is no way to put a value on that gift. What you make of this day, is what matters. God gives the most important gifts in your life. It is up to you what you make of this great gift. Be kind in your words. Be humble in yourself. Do for others without recognition expectations. Start and end you day with a prayer. Be appreciative of your new gift. It is time to get your party started!

December 30:
GOOD MORNING! Can you imagine a world without God? Imagine men (and women) who feel they know everything and they do not care about wrong or right. Imagine a world where laws are created based on men's desires rather than morals, ethics or consequences to others. Imagine a world where people feel the only consequence for their actions will never equal their actions. Imagine a world where God's name is not allowed to be mentioned in schools. Imagine a world where God's image is not allowed in public. Imagine a world where Christian churches are not allowed. Imagine a world where the killing of children is allowed. Imagine a world where men decide who lives or dies. Imagine guidance coming from people with no spiritual belief. Now, imagine coming to the end of your life, in this world, and finding out Heaven and Hell are for real.

December 31:
GOOD MORNING! There will come a time in life when you will lose someone you truly love. There will be those you lose; who shaped your life and effected every bit of who you are. They may pass from this world without any warning. They may linger between death and life for a period of time. They may grow old. They may be a parent, sister, brother, friend, husband, wife, daughter, or son. The pain experienced from the realization of never being

able to speak, touch, see or hear a certain person again can seem to be overwhelming. It may feel like you have lost a part of yourself. The pain may never go away. It will become easier to deal with. Death is final. Once you experience a loss, take the time to think back over the time you spent with that special someone and remember all the good times you had. Remember the times which may have effected you the most and how you became the person you are because of those times. Know that God brought you two together to help you find the person your are now. Now, it is time to grow more. The time will come when you leave this world and others will cry and hurt for your absence. Spend your time with others wisely; and have an appreciation for every moment. There will come a time when that time will be no more. Let others know you care and love them. Never go to bed or leave the house angry. Life is just too short. Thank God you had that special someone in your life; if only briefly.

In closing:

I hope, after you read this; you feel the time was beneficial and enjoyable.

We were all created and designed by God; whether, you believe in Him, or not.

God meant for everyone to be happy and at peace with themselves and the world around them. If you are not; maybe you will find the guidance, and courage you need, to find that happiness within these pages.

My hope for you: is to be at peace with yourself, know you are loved, and know you have a purpose in this world.

You will never be happy with others; unless, you are happy with yourself.

May you be blessed beyond your wishes, dreams and prayers.

Thank you,
Dave

Made in the USA
Columbia, SC
26 March 2021

35070799R00078